DEORTFOLIO

Enh... ...ving Your Stuff

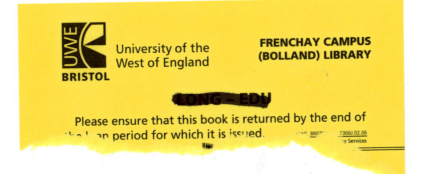

DEVELOPING YOUR PORTFOLIO

Enhancing Your Learning and Showing Your Stuff

A Guide for the Early Childhood Student or Professional

Marianne Jones and Marilyn Shelton

Routledge
Taylor & Francis Group
New York   London

Published in 2006 by
Routledge
Taylor & Francis Group
270 Madison Avenue
New York, NY 10016

Published in Great Britain by
Routledge
Taylor & Francis Group
2 Park Square
Milton Park, Abingdon
Oxon OX14 4RN

Printed in the United States of America on acid-free paper
10 9 8 7 6 5 4 3 2 1

International Standard Book Number-10: 0-415-95117-8 (Hardcover) 0-415-95118-6 (Softcover)
International Standard Book Number-13: 978-0-415-95117-3 (Hardcover) 978-0-415-95118-0 (Softcover)
Library of Congress Card Number 2005008938

Library of Congress Cataloging-in-Publication Data

Jones, Marianne E.
    Developing your portfolio : enhancing your learning and showing your stuff : a guide for the early childhood student or professional / Marianne Jones and Marilyn Shelton.
        p. cm.
    Includes bibliographical references and index.
    ISBN 0-415-95117-8 (hb : alk. paper) -- ISBN 0-415-95118-6 (pb : alk. paper)
    1. Portfolios in education. 2. Early childhood teachers--Training of. I. Shelton, Marilyn R. II. Title.

LB1029.P67J66 2005
372.21--dc22   2005008938

Taylor & Francis Group
is the Academic Division of T&F Informa plc.

Visit the Taylor & Francis Web site at
http://www.taylorandfrancis.com

and the Routledge Web site at
http://www.routledge-ny.com

Contents

Acknowledgments

This has been an amazing journey, and we have some special people to thank. We've been fortunate over the years to have many students who have embraced portfolios, even though they were new to the idea and sometimes anxious about it. We've all been in this together, and we've learned a lot from them about teaching and learning. We appreciate that they have allowed us to include samples of their work and bits of their personal stories about their portfolio journeys. All of this has really enriched us, and the book. We also appreciate the many conference participants who have attended our presentations and graciously given us feedback on our work. Their suggestions and requests for more have inspired us.

Our hats are off to Jeff Jones, whose able-bodied support and generous gift of time pulled us through on more than one occasion. His technical skill, diligence, and long hours at the computer made the manuscript possible. We are eternally grateful.

We want to thank Dr. Bernice Stone, a colleague and friend, for sharing her thoughts on our drafts and sharing her own research on portfolios. Thanks also to our colleague, Chris Henson, for her help with tips on writing conventions.

And finally, we are grateful to our editor, Catherine Bernard. She encouraged us from the beginning of this project to find our own voice. She met our drafts with enthusiasm and a sharp pencil — all of which we appreciate.

Introduction

You know those days when you realize that things are a little out of whack? You scratch your head and wonder what, exactly, is wrong. The disconnect between how early childhood professionals are taught to address children's learning and how adult learning is approached was, for us, one of those head-scratching things. Constructivist practice — hands-on, interactive, social, collaborative — is so engaging. It made us wonder why it is not happening more in classrooms with adult learners. We wanted it to happen more often in our own classrooms. We raised questions for ourselves such as: "How does being prescriptive with students (the paper must be eight pages long; no longer, no shorter) contribute to their critical examination of a topic?" "How can paper-and-pencil tests help students construct knowledge or learn to be self-evaluative or reflective?" We looked again to some of our constructivist beliefs: Adults can construct their own knowledge; they will assume responsibility for their learning if it has meaning to them; and, when given a choice and properly scaffolded, adults prefer active rather than passive learning. If these things are true, as we believe, then we had to structure our classrooms — both the cognitive and emotional aspects — to promote them. We moved increasingly from teacher-directed to student-directed learning. We found that using portfolios with students helped us to do this. Portfolios represent an expression of constructivist learning. They provide an authentic representation of the student's work, learning, and accomplishments.

We've used portfolios with adult learners in child development and early childhood education classes at the community college, baccalaureate, and postbaccalaureate levels over the past 12 years. What we've learned is that it is not easy for students to go from being told how and what to learn to figuring it out for themselves. Over the years we have devised strategies and instruction to help students understand and manage the portfolio process, and keep their sanity. In the process, our guidance and instruction has evolved, and so have we. As we have engaged students in the portfolio process, we have indeed engaged each other in becoming more reflective educators.

In the course of our work, we have read volumes on portfolios, and we have noticed two things. The first is that none really addresses educators across the full spectrum of early care and education — birth through third grade. The second is that none really connects and explains the constructivist underpinnings of portfolios. This book does both.

We have written it for early care and education students and practitioners: those who are in community college and four-year university child development or early childhood education programs or courses, elementary education teacher preparation programs; graduate certificate or master's programs, or working professionals in the field.

This book is both theoretical and practical. The first two chapters set the context for portfolios. The first chapter provides the background, which explains how and why constructivism makes sense in adult learning environments. The second chapter explains the connection between constructivism and portfolios. Chapter 3 begins a thorough, practical discussion of purposes that drive portfolio development, the types of portfolios, the contexts in which they are used, and the audiences to which they are directed. Chapter 4 deals with philosophy and its place in portfolio development and early care and education practice in general. Chapter 5 provides the rationale for the practice of reflection and gives a step-by-step guide to understanding and using it effectively. Chapter 6 covers more of the nitty-gritty of portfolio work. It provides specific guidance about developing, collecting, and evaluating evidence necessary for documenting competency — a big part of what portfolios are about. And last, Chapter 7 addresses the nuts and bolts of portfolio structure, design, and construction — how to show your stuff!

Chapter 1

Human Development and Constructivism

We don't receive wisdom; we must discover it for ourselves after a journey that no one can take for us or spare us.

—Marcel Proust

WHY START A BOOK ABOUT PORTFOLIOS WITH HUMAN DEVELOPMENT AND CONSTRUCTIVISM?

Portfolios are an expression of Constructivism, and Constructivism reflects a certain way of thinking about human learning and development. An understanding of these relationships helps situate portfolios as a tool for learning, for children and adults, a tool that is consistent with best practice in early care and education.

Constructivism is all about authentic learning. It explains how we come to know what we know, what it means to know something, and how our capacity to learn and what we can learn change from one stage of development to another. From an educational standpoint, it helps us understand and create the conditions that encourage and foster authentic learning.

Portfolios represent a window on authentic learning, a tool that reflects the learning process. Portfolios provide a tangible way of making sense of past and present experiences, putting learning in context, and capturing and displaying the learning that has taken place. Portfolios can facilitate authentic learning. They offer a point-in-time portrait of one's development as a learner.

In order to appreciate the power of the portfolio as a tool for learning and development, it is helpful to first understand its theoretical and philosophical foundations — the ideas, really, that underpin it and make it different from traditional forms of assessment. Strong connections exist between Constructivism as a teaching orientation and human development. A brief look at the ideas of the theorists who have so significantly influenced early childhood education provides insights into the use of pedagogy that includes portfolios.

CONSTRUCTIVISM

Understanding what Constructivism is and how it differs from traditional educational philosophy sheds light on some of the difficulties many adult learners and teachers encounter when working with portfolios. It also illuminates some of the reasons that early childhood educators, who practice Constructivism in classrooms with children, have been slow to extend these practices to adult learning environments.

CONSTRUCTIVISM: WHAT IT IS

Constructivism is considered to be a theory by some scholars, an ideology by others. Whatever descriptor you choose, two things are clear. The first is that Constructivism is a particular way of describing the nature of learning and development and how knowledge is acquired. The second is that this particular way of looking at development, learning, and knowing is at the very heart of the early care and education field.

Every discipline, and every theory within a discipline, has its own language. Familiarity with that language aids in formulating a better understanding of it. A close look at the literature on Constructivism reveals the language with which its ideas and concepts are framed and explained. Fosnot's (1996) definition provides an excellent example of the language used to discuss central concepts and ideas embedded in Constructivism. She says, "Constructivism . . . describes knowledge as temporary, developmental, nonobjective, internally constructed, and socially and culturally mediated . . ." (p. ix).

Terms like *temporary*, and *developmental* describe knowledge as something fluid and dynamic, rather than as stagnant and fixed. The words *nonobjective* and *internally constructed* denote the highly personal nature of knowledge and the active processes involved in attaining it. Concurrently, a phrase like *socially and culturally mediated* locates knowledge, and the knower, within the environments in which they live and learn. The social and cultural environments influence, and to some degree, determine or govern, what one knows and how it can be known.

Consider another part of Fosnot's (1996) definition. The language that she uses is instructive in that it clarifies the dynamics involved in learning. She describes learning as

- a self-regulatory process of struggling with the conflict between existing personal models of the world and discrepant new insights,
- constructing new representations and models of reality as a human meaning-making venture with culturally developed tools and symbols, and
- further negotiating such meaning through cooperative social activity, discourse, and debate. (p. ix)

The terms found in this and other descriptions of Constructivism signify an active stance toward learning, suggesting the learners' direct, intentional, purposeful engagement with others and the world around them. Learning is a shared activity, one that demands of us an investment of effort and time.

WHERE CONSTRUCTIVISM COMES FROM

By world history standards, Constructivism is very young. It began in the mid-1800s and is solidly rooted in the work of Froebel, Dewey, Piaget, Vygotsky, and others. Unlike many of their contemporaries, these individuals viewed children as explorers innately disposed to actively construct knowledge and understanding of the world around them. The following brief descriptions of their ideas make clear the influence their thinking has had on early childhood programs around the world. You may recognize in them aspects of programs with which you are familiar.

Friedrich Froebel (1782–1852), influenced by the ideas of Pestalozzi, formulated play-based curriculum through which "children play their way to understanding" (Arnett, 2004, p. 10). Froebel saw children's play as symbolic and developmental, and children as active learners. He believed that "the purpose of education is to encourage and guide man as a conscious, thinking and perceiving being" (Froebel, 1826, p. 2).

John Dewey (1859–1952), the founder of progressive education, argued that children learn by engaging in meaningful, purposeful activity with real objects, doing real-life tasks, rather than by performing abstract tasks for some future purpose. He "advocated intrinsically motivating experiences as essential for the development of a united self and real understanding of subject matter (DeVries & Kohlberg, 1990, p. 376). Dewey believed that the engagement of children's interests, abilities, capabilities, and their active nature are essential to their learning.

Dewey (1933) believed in the power and necessity of reflective thinking, which he considered an essential aim of education and what makes possible "a truly human and rational life" (pp. 17–22). Reflective thinking enables us to act in conscious, mindful ways. It allows us to consider problems and actions systematically. And it enriches and gives meaning to our lives. As with other

Constructivist thinkers, Dewey emphasized active engagement in life and learning.

Piaget (1896–1980), known as the father of Constructivism, provided a theory of how intelligence develops in children and adolescents. He approached intellectual development from the perspective of invariable stage progression. His viewpoint on human development instructs us that human beings progress through specific stages, each stage marked by *a qualitative change in thinking capability*. The four-year-old who reasons that clouds are alive because they move thinks differently than the ten-year-old who knows that a natural force acting on the clouds (wind) causes them to move. The four-year-old generalizes actions of animate and inanimate objects (dogs move; clouds move; dogs are alive, therefore clouds must be alive). The child does not consider the wind to be a factor because the wind is not seen. The 10- to 12-year-old, however, begins to develop the capacity for hypothetical-deductive reasoning and complex and abstract thought. She can consider the nature of physical objects and more readily distinguish between what is alive and what is not. She can comprehend unseen factors, such as gravity or wind, which interact with objects, in ways the younger child cannot. With the help of concrete experiments, she can discover the effects of unseen forces on objects. For example, in a simulation of wind's effects on clouds, the child can use helium balloons tied to the backs of chairs to represent clouds, and moving air produced by a floor fan to represent wind. The child can experiment with the effects of air moving against balloons and mentally apply what she observes to phenomena that she cannot directly experience.

The four-year-old can pretend that balloons are clouds and that the fan is making real wind. Without the cognitive structures of the older child, however, it is just pretend. There is no internalized carryover into reality. The younger child will still believe that clouds move because they are alive. The older child's more mature cognitive structures allow for a different kind of knowing in which the representations and reasoning combine to form new knowledge.

Piaget not only delineated a sequential progression of intellectual development, he explained the process by which children and adolescents learn. He used the term *adaptation* to mean learning and described the two processes that occur in learning. *Assimilation* and *accommodation* are two sides of the learning coin. Assimilation is the taking in of new information and matching it to our existing structures or ways of knowing. Accommodation is what happens when the new information does not fit into our existing mental structures or views. Accommodation requires that we transform our current view in response to the new information. The in-between condition — *disequilibrium* — results when we realize that the new information does not align with our current understanding, and we find ourselves to be temporarily off balance as we struggle to give the new information a home in our view of the world. *Equilibrium* is reached when we successfully integrate the new information, thus creating a new mental construct.

The construction of knowledge and the ideas of assimilation, accommodation, disequilibrium, and equilibrium can be illustrated by the following example.

> *Jill goes to the shoe store to buy a pair of shoes. She asks for her usual size 8. The clerk brings her the size 8, which she tries on and finds to be too small. She asks for another pair, thinking that maybe the first pair was incorrectly marked. The second pair is also too small. Jill decides that that particular style doesn't work for her foot. She asks to see another style, but finds it too small as well. Jill theorizes that shoes from that particular manufacturer must run small, so asks to see other brands of shoes. Size 8 after size 8 proves to be too small, regardless of brand. Still convinced that she wears size 8, Jill applies every reason she can think of to explain why the shoes don't fit. In her attempt to reconcile this experience with her active view ("I'm a size 8"), she rationalizes, "My feet must be swollen," "It's late in the day so I must be retaining water," or "They just don't make them like they used to."*

In an effort to make sense of this experience and match it with what she knows, she calls upon her known theories to explain it. Piaget and Inhelder (1969) describe this as assimilation, "The filtering or modification of the input" (p. 6). In other words, Jill does her best to assimilate the fact of the shoes not fitting into her current belief about her shoe size and tries to justify why she's having trouble with the size 8s.

When at last, Jill cannot find a single, comfortable size 8, she's faced with having to change her mind about her shoe size. She tries on size 9 and finds that it fits perfectly. She accommodates her thinking to the current experience. Piaget and Inhelder (1969) describe this as "the modification of internal schemes to fit reality" (p. 6). This experience causes Jill to rethink her old view and create a new view. The interaction of assimilation and accommodation effectively *changes her mind*, resulting in *adaptation* (learning).

Like Dewey, Piaget believed that the construction of knowledge requires action on the part of the learner. Children do not learn from objects; rather, they learn by *acting on* objects, observing the results of those actions, and then trying to make sense of what they see. Piaget believed that the sense that children can make of their experience is limited by their stage of intellectual development. A thorough discussion of Piaget's developmental stages is beyond the scope of this book. However, we will touch on the stage Formal Operations later in this chapter in a discussion of adult learning.

Piaget primarily emphasized the *actions of the individual* in the learning process. Although he acknowledged the importance of social interaction in the construction of knowledge, it was his contemporary, Lev Vygotsky (1896–1934), who brought Social Constructivism to the forefront. Vygotsky insisted that the construction of knowledge always exists within the context of past and present social relationships. In his view, learning occurs through intentional and purposeful engagement *with more knowledgeable and experienced others* while acting on the environment. Learning and development are conditioned on human interaction and shared activity in the physical environment. As Badrova and Leong (1996) point out:

> "The social context molds cognitive processes, while it is also part of the developmental process. Social context means the entire social milieu, that is, everything in the child's environment that has either been directly or indirectly influenced by the culture" (p. 9).

Vygotsky's placement of learning and development in the sociocultural context resonates with the ideas of Bronfenbrenner (1917–), who sets human development within the context of an ecological system. In Bronfenbrenner's model, the child is, first and foremost, part of a microsystem — the family. Each individual and each relationship within the family affects the others. As the child develops, he experiences the larger environment — the meso-system — in which he, and his family members, interact with, for example, extended family, child care, school, the neighborhood, and the church. The relationships represented in these and other microsystems directly influence the child's development and worldview. In less direct ways, yet important ones, the child is affected by elements in the exosystem, such as the parents' work, the school board, government agencies, the legal system, and other entities with which family members have contact. And finally, the child is influenced, again indirectly, by the macrosystem, or global context, which includes, for instance, cultural customs, social class, historical events, and popular ideologies.

THE OTHER SIDE OF HUMAN DEVELOPMENT

Constructivism tells an important story about the social and cognitive aspects of, and conditions for, learning. It is not the whole story, however. The Child Study Movement, begun by G. Stanley Hall (1846–1924), "was dedicated to creating a scientific approach to understanding child development" (Frost, Wortham, & Reifel, 2005, p. 14). The idea of the *whole child* was born in that movement, and it forms an important part of the foundation on which Constructivism is built. The concept of the *whole person* — both the cognitive and affective aspects — has been fundamental to the larger study of human development.

While Dewey, Piaget, and others were busy investigating cognitive development and learning, Sigmund Freud (1856–1939) was revolutionizing the way we think about the structure and development of the psyche or mental life of the person. He hypothesized that the psyche is made up of three interacting aspects: *id* — our instincts; *ego* — "the intermediary between id and the external world" (Strachey, 1969, p. 2); and *superego* — our conscience. Freud illuminated the workings of the unconscious mind — our motivations, drives, interpretations of reality, and desires — which influence our conscious and unconscious choices throughout life.

The theories of Freud and his student, Eric Erikson (1902–1994), have provided insights into the development and functioning of the affective domain. They identified psychosexual and psychosocial stages, respectively, through which individuals internalize and make emotional and social-psychological sense out of their experiences. Our interpretations of the experiences in each stage provide either a healthy foundation for development that continues with us throughout life, or one that is, to some degree, compromised. The extent to which we successfully resolve the issues in each stage affects the quality and stability of the stages that follow, and have a consequent effect on the quality of our lives and subsequent relationships. These theories address the effects of the individual's *personal interactions* with significant others within each stage. For instance, during infancy, the quality of the infant's life experience depends on the mother's level and quality of responsiveness to the infant's needs. Healthy development requires that the infant's efforts to communicate be met with timely, nurturing, appropriate responses. A consistent pattern of responsiveness convinces the infant on an unconscious level that the world is a safe place, that relationships are satisfying, that she is competent to communicate her needs, and that her needs will be met. In Erikson's (1963) terms, she forms a basic sense of trust, rather than one of mistrust. It is postulated that these formative experiences throughout childhood have a profound impact on our adult lives, influencing everything from the spouse we choose to the feelings and thoughts we experience when we enter a room full of strangers.

When viewed in combination, this sample of theories presents a picture of development that views the human being as possessing both a conscious and unconscious mind, which is shaped through a combination of genetic endowments and direct and indirect social experiences. Each domain interacts with and affects the development of the other; each is important to healthy development. Individual strengths and challenges are manifested in various ways and are influenced by a multitude of personal and environmental factors. Our emotional and cognitive lives are intertwined. Piaget and Inhelder (1969) noted the reciprocal and inseparable nature of our cognitive and affective sides. They concluded that every pattern of behavior, no matter how intellectual, is always influenced to some degree by our affective states. Conversely, our affective states have voice — in fact, exist — as a result of our cognitive structures. This holds true for both children and adults.

Much of the early care and education field reflects these Constructivist, psychodynamic, and ecological views of learning and development. We can see the reflections of Dewey, Piaget, Vygotsky, Freud, Erikson, Bronfenbrenner, and others in our field in how we view young children, and in how these views are expressed in high-quality early childhood programs. Early childhood educators respect children's capacities and emerging capabilities. We view their learning as a complex, personal, and interpersonal endeavor with both emotional and cognitive content. We give children opportunities, in a social context, to express and examine their thoughts and knowledge about the world as they experience it. Against the backdrop of their understanding and capabilities at a given time, we engage them with new opportunities that challenge and invite them to try out, and think about, their thinking and actions in response to what they have learned — to continually transform their knowledge in synchrony with their expanding capabilities. We also take into consideration their feelings, motivations, desires, and psychological needs. Learning requires that children actively engage in a potent, circular process that includes action on objects and ideas, interaction with more knowledgeable others, and reflection and dialogue on their thinking and actions in supportive environments. We understand children's learning as a transformative process. This is not only true for children, however. It is also true for adults. Why, then, do we so rarely find constructivist ideas and practices at work in adult learning environments?

WHY OUR TEACHING PRACTICES IN ADULT LEARNING ENVIRONMENTS OFTEN DO NOT REFLECT OUR CONSTRUCTIVIST BELIEFS

Although many early childhood educators share these human development views and embrace and practice Constructivism with children, there has been a long-standing disconnect in the early care and education field between how we teach adults and how we teach adults to work with children. Two factors may explain the pervasive disconnect that results in the perpetuation of *teaching as telling* in the adult classroom.

The first factor has its roots in the history of our educational system. Our educational institutions are historically underpinned by a philosophical ideology referred to as *cultural transmission,* which stems from the Behaviorist tradition. Prior to the 1800s, conventional wisdom held that children were—empty vessels to be filled up by adults. John Locke (1632–1704) wrote, "the mind of a newborn infant is like a blank page upon which experience writes" (Harriman, 1941, pp. 180–181). Locke coined the phrase *tabula rosa* to describe this idea. *Tabula rosa* is associated with Behaviorism wherein it is believed that experience *acts on the child* to produce learning. In this view, knowledge results when information comes from the outside to the inside through the senses. External stimuli govern what can be known, and therefore, learned (DeVries & Kohlberg, 1990). Behaviorism acknowledges only that which comes from outside the person, that which is observable and measurable. It makes no allowance for the unseen mental activity of the person through which one *acts on, shapes, comprehends, invents, and makes meaning from and within* one's environment and experience. Harriman (1941) illustrates this Behaviorist premise as he explains, "If the infant were incapable of receiving and responding to stimuli, and of acquiring new modes of responses, there would be nothing of what we call mind or mental development" (p. 182).

In the cultural transmission view, children learn by having adults transmit information to them; this is a view that sees children as passive receptacles who take as their own, without question or reflection, that which others know, say, or believe. If we consider the cultural transmission ideology — which conceives of learning as a passive activity — we can see that it is an approach that persists in much of elementary, secondary, and adult education. Hillocks (1999) describes this passive approach as an *objectivist stance* to teaching, that is, ". . . teaching . . . as an act of telling" (p. 93). With such an approach, it is not difficult to understand why the lecture method is so common in our collective school experience. It makes sense if learning is thought of as an exercise in filling the heads of students with information poured from the mouths of teachers. It also assumes that information is something to be wholly transmitted, static and permanent by nature, requiring nothing more than absorption on the part of the learner.

Through our extensive personal experiences in school, we have each formed beliefs and theories about the nature of teaching and learning. These beliefs and theories contain powerful, enduring ideas about authority relationships, teachers' roles and responsibilities, pedagogy, and the roles we, and our peers, play in relation to our learning. If we predominantly experienced traditional methods of education, chances are good that we hold the unconscious, fundamental assumptions that teachers possess knowledge and then transmit it to students (Bullard, 2003), that learning occurs through the passive transfer of knowledge from teacher to student, and that students are the recipients of that knowledge "who perform according to the teachers' expectations" (Burk & Dunn, 1996, p. 11). Motivation for learning results from the external rewards bestowed on the student by the teacher. These rewards most often take the form of grades.

If we experienced a passive educational approach as our primary mode of instruction, then it may be the mode that "feels right" to us, even though we might have experienced it as ineffective — that is, the information we heard did not stick. As teachers, we have often heard students say, "I learned it for the test. As soon as the test was over, I forgot everything." In spite of this fairly constant refrain, educators of adults persist in using a passive approach, because it is, after all, what we know, and that with which we are most comfortable. Bullard (2003) cites extensive research that confirms that the personal theories learners hold about teaching and learning, their beliefs about the proper roles of teachers and students, and the ideas they maintain about the right way to teach and learn are, indeed, highly resistant to change. Furthermore, these beliefs act as a filter when a learner is confronted with new ways of doing things, often confounding the possibility of change.

A second factor that may contribute to early childhood educators' perpetuation of *teaching as telling* is how we have understood and interpreted Piaget's stage of Formal Operations. As stated previously, Piaget was a stage theorist. He believed that children mature into each of four stages — formal operations being the last — and that each stage builds upon those that precede it. No stage can be skipped. Each stage is marked by distinct states of intellectual capability. Developing intellect is not a matter of learning more; it is a matter of growing the capability for more sophisticated thought processes. In other words, the way that children are able to think is fundamentally different from the way adults are able to think.

So how might our interpretation of this stage contribute to *teaching as telling*? The hallmark of Piaget's stage of Formal Operations is the development of capabilities for abstract and complex thought, metacognition (thinking about thinking), and hypothetical-deductive reasoning (Arnett, 2004). In Formal Operations, ideas, rather than concrete objects, become the prominent currency. We know that both language and ideas are abstract, and inextricably linked. Many of us have been taught that *all* adolescents and adults achieve, and engage in, Formal Operations as a matter of inevitable stage progression, as Piaget suggested. If we believe that all adolescents and adults think in abstract and complex ways, and that they understand language — a system of abstract symbols that conveys meaning — then why would not we also believe that these learners can absorb and understand, by being "told," what we expect them to know?

These two factors — our experiences as passive learners and our beliefs about how adults learn — conspire to keep us blind to change. They keep our *quiet theories* about education, internalized through years of experience, in place. It is those quiet theories that provide our personal recipes for educational practice. The most common recipe in our schools today is based on the notion of passing on wholly formed knowledge to students, who learn, not through action and social interaction, but instead through rote memorization and didactic instructional methods.

The Constructivist view of learning invites us to challenge our quiet theories about teaching and learning. Arnett (2004) cites abundant research that gives us a revised view of Piaget's stage of Formal Operations. That research indicates that, rather than a certainty into which all people mature, Formal Operations is a universal potential that all people possess. That potential is realized and exercised differently in different cultures. The ways in which it is developed and exercised is determined by the cognitive tasks on which individual cultures depend. People tend to exercise their capability for abstract and complex thought selectively, often with problems with which they are most familiar or with which they have the most experience. People who have had systematic or specialized training are more likely than others to develop their capabilities for abstract and complex thought. Those who develop these capabilities often use them selectively or inconsistently. Some fail to exercise this level of thought at all. In short, we must be taught to think abstractly and reflectively, engage in guided practice to become proficient, and exert considerable effort and energy to exercise this kind of thinking effectively in our daily lives.

In describing a Constructivist stance toward teaching and learning, Hillocks (1999) says, "Teachers cannot simply tell students what is to be learned and expect them to learn it . . . students must themselves be active agents in their own learning, transforming what is to be learned through the screen of their own experience and existing understandings . . . to be successful, learners must construct or reconstruct, for themselves, what is to be learned" (p. 93). We contend that this is true for both the child and the adult learner.

HOW CONSTRUCTIVISM APPLIES
TO ADULT LEARNERS

Early childhood educators have focused primarily on how Constructivism applies to children and on how to put into operation Constructivist ideas to build meaningful curriculums in children's programs. A great deal has been written about adult development, learning, and education, and the connections among them, in the past few decades, however. Educators such as Mezirow and Associates (1990, 1991, 2000), Brookfield (1986, 1987, 1995, 1996), and Candy (1991) have echoed the ideas of the early Constructivists and extended Constructivist principles to adult environments. These prominent adult educators view learning as potentially emancipatory and transformative. Their work, and that of others in the field of adult education, is replete with references to active learning, self-direction, and intrinsic motivation.

Our own experiences with a wide variety of adults and children in diverse learning environments have taught us that Constructivism, and the pedagogical practices that it suggests, apply equally well to students of any age. As with children, adults tend to thrive in settings that invite and value their active, purposeful participation, and where learning is a shared responsibility. Most adults respond to an atmosphere of inquiry, wherein their questions about, and exploration of, the world and themselves are encouraged. We have discovered that high-level learning is most likely to occur when teachers and students engage, with open minds, in productive and energetic dialogue and meaningful tasks that address real problems.

Constructivism has given us an alternative to the cultural transmission approach to learning. In doing so, it gives us guidance as to the role of education. Daloz (1999) says, "The proper aim of education is to promote significant learning. Significant learning entails development. Development means successively asking broader and deeper questions of the relationship between oneself and the world" (p 3). The connection that Daloz makes between learning and development is a crucial one, but to early childhood educators, not an unfamiliar one. If Daloz were talking in Piagetian terms, she would be discussing the process of assimilation and accommodation, which results in adaptation (learning). As you recall, in this process, we first try to interpret new information using our existing ways of knowing. Upon finding the existing structures inadequate, we construct a new way of understanding and making sense of the experience — our ways of knowing are transformed. The adult learning literature underscores and corroborates Piaget's analysis of how learning happens, not only in children, but in adults as well. Ultimately, what Piaget described is the process of *transformative human* learning.

The Constructivist view of learning moves us from a perspective of learning as *transfer of information* to one of learning as *transformation of information*. An educational approach that is built on *information transfer* often results in surface learning and an assortment of discrete bits of information with a short shelf life. For example, most of us took a course in geometry in high school. We were instructed to memorize theorem after theorem. We may have done so and successfully passed every exam. Can we recall and employ a single one when trying to figure out how many square feet an odd-shaped piece of ground contains when planning the school garden?

On the other hand, an educational approach built on *information transformation* has the potential for resulting in deep-level learning with staying power. Why? Because when we transform information, truly learn it, we make it our own. It becomes knowledge. If we had really learned the theorems in geometry class, rather than temporarily memorized them, we would understand their underlying principles and the processes through which they were derived. We would have made sense of them by struggling with their meaning, applying them in varied circumstances, observing and analyzing our results, and sharing and comparing the results with others. Through this active, involved collaborative process, we would have altered our pretheorem world understanding to a more enlightened one that includes our working knowledge of theorems as a way of understanding how the world operates. That transformed information — knowledge — would then be available to us when planning the school garden!

IMPLICATIONS FOR THE ADULT LEARNING ENVIRONMENT

Constructivist principles orient us toward a dynamic educational environment for adult learners. As educators of adults, our desire to reinvent our teaching in ways that bring what we do, what we know, and what we believe into harmony has given us the courage and impetus to experiment, reflect, engage in dialogue, study, and experiment some more. We have recognized that upsetting the apple cart, so to speak, has risks for us as teachers and for our students as well. Not only have we experienced the discomfort of jarring our own ideas about teaching and learning, but we have also encountered resistance and anxiety in our students as we bring Constructivist principles to bear in our classrooms. To some extent, we are all prisoners of our *quiet theories*. On the printed page, the idea of *cognitive conflict* or *dissonance* sounds rather benign and intellectual. In practice, it often causes emotional and intellectual confusion, rebellion, foot-dragging, avoidance, and anger in students. Most of them rise to the challenge. Many times, students embrace the adventure and engage wholeheartedly, becoming learning partners with us in the coconstruction of knowledge. Our efforts to operationalize Constructivism in the adult classroom continue to inform our practice as teachers, and open cognitive doors for adult learners that help them transform their thinking, knowing, and doing. We see this when they grapple with issues, scaffold one another's learning, try out and analyze new approaches to old problems, and reflect on their efforts and progress. We see the practice of Constructivist principles come to life when they make visible what they know, how they know it, what they can do, and what it all means to them.

In the next chapter, we explore Constructivism as it relates specifically to portfolios. Our journeys to discovering better ways to teach have brought us, by different paths, to portfolios. In them, we have found more than the stories of students' learning. We have found an important part of our Constructivist selves.

A FINAL NOTE

Constructivism is at the heart of early care and education. If offers a holistic view of human learning and development, considering the cognitive, social, and affective aspects of the learner. Although, in our field, we characteristically apply Constructivist principles and practices to working with children, we have not always extended these to adult learning. The theoretical basis and implications for practice embedded in Constructivism apply equally well to both children and adults.

Chapter 2

How Portfolios Reflect Constructivism

The self is not something ready-made, but something in continuous formation through choice of action.

—John Dewey

CONSTRUCTIVISM AND PORTFOLIOS

In traditional schooling, emphasis has been placed squarely, and almost exclusively, on development in the cognitive domain. Educators expend proportionately little energy, in an intentional, concerted way, on development in the affective and social domains. The single-minded focus on logical-mathematical and linguistic skills, and the testing that accompanies it, might lead one to believe that knowing facts and learning to manage, process, and express information makes for an educated person. Behaviorism, so deeply ingrained in our education system, undergirds this view. While there is no question that cognitive skill-building and retaining information are important, they represent only one dimension of learning. Hutchings and Wutzdorff (1988) describe learning, in part, as involving and engaging a range of domains, including the cognitive, kinesthetic, affective, ethical, attitudinal, and behavioral. As educators, if we recognize the logical-mathematical and linguistic biases embedded in our educational institutions, and perhaps in our own quiet theories, and we begin to think about learning as going beyond these dimensions of cognition, then we must ask ourselves what else is important in adult learning, and how is it realized? These are some of the connections and questions we continually consider as we reflect on our practice with adult learners.

In order to bring about change, we had to reexamine what we believe about how people develop and learn. We challenged our own theories about education and educational practice. We wanted an approach wherein the learning and developmental needs of the whole person are considered. It meant moving away from a didactic stance — *teaching as telling — learning as receiving* into a position of *facilitator of learning and development — active participant*. The *teaching as telling — learning as receiving approach* is conducive to the idea of "knowledge as facts." A *facilitator of learning and development — active participant approach* invites a different understanding of knowledge, and a different approach to knowledge-building. It is one that treats education as a partnership. It is respectful of what the learner, as well as the teacher, brings to the educational environment. It includes both the cognitive and affective aspects of the learner.

Through his theory of Multiple Intelligences, Howard Gardner (1983) introduced the idea that intelligence is not limited to the logical-mathematical or linguistic arenas. Rather, intelligence finds expression in a variety of "frames of mind" that also include the musical, kinesthetic, naturalistic, spatial, intrapersonal, and interpersonal (p. 8). Daniel Goleman (1995) argues that emotional intelligence contributes immeasurably to human success. The emotional mind and the rational mind, he explains, present "two fundamentally different ways of knowing [which] interact to construct our mental life" (p. 8). Often, he says, "these minds are exquisitely coordinated; feelings are essential to thought, thought to feeling" (p. 9). Emotional intelligence encompasses empathy, self-awareness, personal motivation, and a host of other aspects that enable us to engage with ourselves and with others to succeed in personal relationships, work, and play. Our experience has taught us that it is not enough to engage our adult students cognitively. As Mezirow and Associates (2000) point out, "transformative learning is more than rationally based; it relies on the affective dimension of knowing . . ." (p. 303).

A teaching/learning approach that takes into account the cognitive, social, and affective dimensions of the learner necessitates the use of tools, methods, and strategies that go well beyond the standard paper-and-pencil tests and the traditional emphasis on "producing the right answer." Examination of our practice prompted us to explore alternative approaches that would facilitate, in adult learners, the messy kind of learning we observe in young children — exploratory, inventive, insightful, and productive. We wanted to find ways to engage adult learners in developing competencies, enabling them "*to resolve genuine problems or difficulties* . . . to create an effective product [that entails] the potential for *finding or creating problems* — thereby laying the groundwork for the acquisition of new knowledge" (Gardner, 1983, pp. 60–61). We were seeking to engage students in what Fosnot (1996) describes as "an interpretive, recursive, building process by active learners interacting with the physical and social world" (p. 30). Portfolios provided us with a powerful strategy and tool with which to engage students.

Figure 2-1 illustrates the alignments between theory and practice with which we struggled to arrive at internal congruence and consistency in our

CONCEPTUAL ALIGNMENT

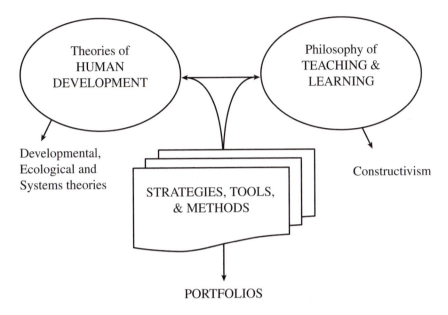

Figure 2-1. Conceptual Alignment.

teaching. It shows the interplay between theories (how people learn and develop) and philosophy (beliefs and values about how best to educate them). Pedagogy (how teachers teach) emanates from theories and beliefs. If theories and beliefs are aligned, pedagogical choices tend to be more clear and consistent. In fact, theoretical and philosophical groundings influence pedagogical approach. In our case, bringing our theories and philosophy into alignment caused us to reframe our pedagogy. Portfolios emerged as a pedagogical response to that realignment. This is the same alignment struggle we have observed taking place in our adult students as they move through the portfolio process. In effect, the portfolio process has set up the dynamic, whereby students are called to question their theories, beliefs, and practices.

OUR JOURNEY TO PORTFOLIOS: A CONSTRUCTIVIST STORY

The past few decades have seen a dramatic increase in the use of portfolios in schools of education to assess the preparation of elementary, middle, and secondary school teachers, and also at the college and university levels as tools for determining readiness for tenure and promotion. Although early childhood educators have become accustomed to using portfolios in their classrooms to document children's growth and development, portfolios are much less often used with adult learners in early childhood course preparation and continuing education programs. We find this particularly curious, in that, as previously noted, early childhood educators have long been committed to the Constructivist philosophy in working with children. Constructivism has been an ideal in early care and education to a much greater degree, and for a much longer time, than at any other level of American education.

It is clear from our observations of good early childhood practice that early childhood educators, in the spirit of Constructivism, understand and respond to the uneven growth and development patterns in young children. They expect and plan for the messiness of children's learning. They encourage their creativity, actively engage them, challenge them, and scaffold their learning, and consider both their cognitive and affective needs. Educators sometimes forget, however, that all of these things also apply when dealing with adult learners.

WHAT ARE PORTFOLIOS?

There are many definitions of portfolios in the education literature (Brown & Wolfe-Quintero, 1997; Campbell, Cignetti, Melenyz, Nettles, & Wyman, 2004; Cerbin, 1994; Paulson, Paulson, & Meyer, 1991; Wolf & Dietz, 1998; Wolf, Lichtenstein & Stevenson, 1997). They generally characterize portfolios as organized or structured collections of work compiled for a specific purpose related to the demonstration of one's learning, skills, and accomplishments. Most of the definitions refer only to the portfolio product — that is, the end result of a series of steps. Others make explicit the process aspect of portfolio development — process as it relates to personal change (McMillan, 2004; Wilcox, 1996; Wolf & Dietz, 1998). Some of the definitions emphasize the role of reflection in portfolios (Wolf & Dietz, 1998; Wolf et al., 1997), while others are silent on this point.

As we have come to better understand the complexity of portfolios through our work with students, our definition has evolved. In it, we have tried to capture both the process and the product dimensions of portfolios, which we see as being intertwined and complementary. The process that underlies port-folio development is as important as the product itself, as it is through the process that learning occurs. The quality and depth of the process is reflected in the product, and ultimately determines the quality of the product. This, then, is our definition:

> Portfolios are rich, contextual, highly personalized documentaries of one's learning journey. They contain purposefully organized documentation that clearly demonstrates specific knowledge, skills, dispositions and accomplishments achieved over time. Portfolios represent connections made between actions and beliefs, thinking and doing, and evidence and criteria. They are a medium for reflection through which the builder constructs meaning, makes the learning

process transparent and learning visible, crystallizes insights, and anticipates future direction.

Portfolios represent both an expression of Constructivist learning and a vehicle for Constructivist practice. Portfolios are the embodiment of holistic learning. The process learners experience in developing portfolios, and the products that result, allow them, and invite them, to give voice to their cognitive, social, and affective selves. Portfolios are portraits of their builders.

Portfolios lend themselves to a variety of uses that we will discuss in later chapters. In all cases, however, they facilitate learners' exploring of questions and addressing of problems that are complex, multifaceted, reflective of builders' value systems, and embedded in the sociocultural environment. Portfolios represent an approach to learning wherein the "right answer" is not the teacher's answer, but rather one constructed by the learner in dialogue with others.

CHARACTERISTICS OF PORTFOLIOS

All portfolios hold several characteristics in common. We briefly discuss each of these characteristics below with a reference to where in the book we cover them in detail.

Clearly Specified Purpose and Audience

The purpose and audience of the portfolio must be clearly defined and understood. Purpose and audience guide the builder in decision making with regard to collection, use, and presentation of evidence. Purpose and audience suggest the type of portfolio that is most appropriate and may indicate a particular structural design. We cover purpose and audience in detail in Chapter 3.

Philosophy Statement

All portfolios contain some form of philosophy statement. This carefully crafted statement unifies all elements within the portfolio. It embodies one's beliefs and values, which underpin and center the process. Chapter 4 discusses philosophy statements in detail.

Reflections

Reflection is the defining characteristic of portfolios. None is complete without it. It is what separates a portfolio from a scrapbook. Reflections tie artifacts to learning and provide evidence of growth and change over time. Reflection is covered in detail in Chapter 5.

Evidence

Evidence must be carefully selected and suited to the portfolio's purpose. Selecting documentation is akin to furnishing a room. If done poorly, without planning and reflection, the room can look like grandma's unkempt attic. If done well, it can convey a sense of balance, harmony, style, and substance — a place where one (the reader) would want to spend time. Evidence is addressed in depth in Chapter 6.

Structural Design

Structural design is all about the packaging of the final product. It involves such issues as format and organization of the document as a whole. The decisions you make here will determine how the work is received and will allow your personality to shine through. Structural design is discussed in detail in Chapter 7.

BENEFITS OF PORTFOLIO DEVELOPMENT

In our experience, portfolio development has benefited adult learners in some significant ways. First, the portfolio process helps students to reframe how they see themselves as learners. It empowers individuals to take responsibility for their learning — to examine previously passive roles and to become more proactive in their learning endeavors. It encourages them to think about their learning, and the learning environment, in critical and meaningful ways — to become mindful, intentional, self-directed learners. For many learners, the portfolio process reignites their intellectual curiosity, the same quality we admire and seek to foster in children.

Second, the portfolio process provokes adult learners to look at education differently — as integrative and ongoing — reaching far beyond the confines of the classroom and continuing throughout life. We have heard so often from students over the years that they have felt that their college classes were irrelevant and had no connection to "real life." Many have experienced higher education as a series of hoops one jumps through to get the "piece of paper." On the contrary, students who have experienced the portfolio process report a high degree of connectedness between what they do in the college classroom what they experience beyond the classroom door. The real-world nature of portfolio work bridges the theory-to-practice gap in ways that result in meaningful learning and change. Course content ceases to be the stuff one crams for a test and soon forgets. It comes to be owned by the learner, and therefore it becomes part of the fabric of one's professional life and development.

Third, portfolio development encourages meaningful, rather than rote, learning. This kind of learning rarely happens in a straight line. It involves inevitable twists and turns, requires backsteps, and goes around corners only to confront and challenge the learner in new and unexpected ways. It is the messy kind of learning that requires all of us, teachers and students, to think about and question what we know, how we know it, and how it affects us, and it requires that we engage in dialogue about these things together. Grant and Huebner (1998) call this "powerful learning . . . active and relevant. In teacher education, as in all educational settings, powerful learning happens when what is learned and how it is learned are organized to build on the strengths of the learner" (pp. 33–34). Fink (2003) calls it significant learning.

Fink (2003) has provided a taxonomy of significant learning that we think finds expression in the process of portfolio development, and in the product itself. He describes significant learning experiences as those that have "both a *process* and an *outcome* dimension" (p. 6). In his view, and ours, significant learning results in lasting change that the learner interprets as important and meaningful in his personal or professional life. Fink identifies six kinds of significant learning that involve the cognitive, social, and emotional domains: foundational knowledge, application, integration, human dimension, caring, and learning how to learn (p. 30). Figure 2-2 provides our interpretation of his taxonomy as we use it with our students.

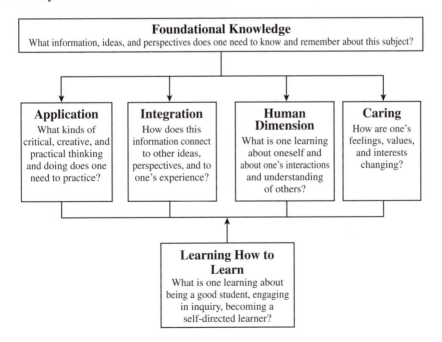

Figure 2-2. Taxonomy of Significant Learning.

As Fink (2003) points out,

> One important feature of this taxonomy is that it is not hierarchical but rather relational and even interactive . . . each kind of learning is related to the other kinds of learning and . . . achieving any one kind of learning simultaneously enhances the possibility of achieving the other kinds of leaning as well (p. 32).

Notice that the process begins with foundational knowledge — what one sets out to learn, for example, about the relationship between child development, play, and learning. It is not enough to learn the names of Smilansky's play states in children from birth to age five. The other kinds of learning — application, integration, the human dimension, and caring — are the aspects that help transform the information into personal knowledge that has meaning. The ability to apply the knowledge — to recognize solitary play and differentiate it from parallel play while observing a group of children — provides new tools that help one be more effective in designing play opportunities and in being more responsive to children's individual play needs. Integrating our understanding of block play and our knowledge of how children develop spatial reasoning and literacy enlarges one's repertoire of curriculum tools. Looking closely at children's play in relation to their development gives one an opportunity to examine one's beliefs and attitudes about the importance and purpose of play. This human dimension of learning gives insights into the messages one gives parents, children, and others about the place play has in education. The caring aspect of learning invites us to fall in love with a subject like play, or perhaps come to value it in a way previously unfelt. And finally, experiencing learning in this holistic way opens the door to more self-directed learning.

As Fink points out, learning is interconnected. An interactive, relational approach predisposes consideration of both the cognitive and affective domains in the learning process. Portfolios engage students by invoking their cognitive and affective involvement.

Fourth, our experience has shown that portfolio development strengthens formal operational thought processes — metacognition, abstract and complex thought, and hypothetical-deductive reasoning. It provides not only a means for internalizing learning at deeper levels, but also a means for developing and/or refining higher order thinking skills. As pointed out in Chapter 1, higher order skills, characteristic of the formal operations stage of development, do not just happen. They are realized through a combination of an individual's cognitive readiness, systematic instruction, and guided practice, along with an individual's personal effort. Grant and Huebner (1998) point out that "Learning with understanding is more likely when one is required to explain, elaborate, or defend one's position to others, as well as one's self . . ." (p. 35). Portfolios necessitate a complex interplay of activities in which the learner is constantly striving to explain, elaborate, and defend. They provide a vehicle through which learners transform information and experience into new knowledge that becomes their own, and think contextually about thinking and learning in increasingly complex ways.

Fifth, portfolio development facilitates self-awareness and discovery. It encourages learners to express what they know and can do in personally meaningful, individualized, and creative ways. Portfolios accommodate multiple ways of knowing and acknowledge the full range of learning styles. Portfolios often validate learners' knowledge and skills, encouraging them to reflect on, recognize, evaluate, and appreciate their own progress. They are a vehicle for refining professional identity and recording ongoing growth, and they provide a source of pride for the builder.

CHALLENGING ASPECTS
OF PORTFOLIO DEVELOPMENT

Portfolio development presents adult learners with a variety of challenges. First, it is time consuming. The concept of adult portfolios is new to many students and consequently takes time to fully understand. Portfolios require considerable planning, collection and development of evidence, organization, and assembly — all of which take time. They demand a high degree of stick-to-itiveness, self-pacing, follow-through, and attention to detail.

Second, for many students, portfolios can be anxiety producing, at least initially. The highly individualized nature of portfolios makes them unlike most other kinds of assignments with which students are familiar. They represent a shift from teacher-directed to student-directed learning that can cause psychological disequilibrium — a quake in one's quiet theories about teachers' and students' roles in the learning environment and what learning is. A certain measure of discomfort accompanies any significant learning, any significant shift in how one experiences learning, and any significant shift in external expectations surrounding learning. The disequilibrium that these shifts bring about, however, also creates the possibility for substantive growth and change.

Third, portfolio development can be unsettling because it requires reconsideration of one's thinking about the nature and purpose of adult learning. What early childhood educators believe about children's learning — that it is a messy, uneven process that requires tenacity — is also true for adults. Instead of messing around with sand and water, adults mess around with ideas. The process is the same; only the medium has changed. It takes a while to get back in the habit of being curious, inventive, and intuitive where learning is concerned. It takes time, effort, and trust to unlearn years of passivity — to go from "What does the teacher want?" to "What will help me develop as a professional?"

And finally, portfolio development challenges adult learners to develop, and then utilize and trust, their own instincts and judgment. Instincts and judgment must be exercised in a whole range of decisions, such as what artifact is meaningful and important in relation to a particular criterion, when is something enough or too much, what constitutes quality, and how can one best project professionalism.

The challenges students face in developing portfolios may seem daunting at first. The anxiety, confusion, and uncertainty students sometimes feel are certainly very real, and very predictable. It has been our experience, however, and students have reported to us, that the benefits far outweigh the negatives. The autonomy students feel, the uniqueness of each student's experience, and the true sense of ownership and accomplishment that comes with the portfolio territory makes it all worth it in the end. For many, it is truly a transforming experience.

A FINAL NOTE

Portfolios open a window into the learning process. They offer a dynamic alternative to more traditional approaches to learning. They give students opportunities to explore and experiment with real-world problems and demonstrate what they know and can do. Without a doubt, portfolios are time consuming and require a great deal of effort to do well, but the outcome — and the learning that results from it — are lasting.

Chapter 3

Portfolio Orientation: Purpose, Type, Context, and Audience

Learning is not attained by chance, it must be sought for with ardor and attended to with diligence.

—Abigail Adams

Just as an architect must "get the lay of the land" before planning a structure and laying the first brick, the portfolio builder must understand the orientation before embarking on the building of a portfolio. Orientation refers to the portfolio's purpose, the context in which it will be used, the type of portfolio best suited to the purpose, and the intended audience. Purpose, type, context, and audience set the orientation of the portfolio and give the builder direction.

In our review of the literature on portfolios, we have found that the terms *purpose, type*, and *audience* are often confused, lumped together, or used interchangeably. The idea of *context* is rarely addressed. In our work, we have given each of these terms specific meaning as they relate to this notion of portfolio orientation. We distinguish between the *purposes* for which portfolios are developed, the *types* of portfolios one might develop, the *audiences* to whom they are directed, and the *contexts* in which they are commonly employed, as these are not the same.

PURPOSE, TYPE, CONTEXT, AND AUDIENCE: WHAT IS THE DIFFERENCE?

We think about portfolios in this way: One develops a particular type of portfolio to achieve a specific purpose within a context that includes an identified audience. Purpose and type are closely related, as are context and audience.

Purpose answers the question "Why am I doing this?" It is the reason for which a portfolio is created. Purpose is central to everything that follows in both development and design of a portfolio. Purpose determines the type of portfolio to be developed and indicates the likely audience to whom it will be directed.

Type answers the question "What kind of portfolio is best suited to the purpose?" The type of portfolio you develop flows directly from its purpose. We distinguish four basic types of portfolios, as we use them. These types are developmental, showcase, assessment, and professional portfolios.

Context answers the question "How and where will I use it?" We define *contexts* as the circumstances or situations in which portfolios are used. For instance, you may develop a portfolio as a course or program requirement wherein the instructor directs and guides the process and sets the parameters.

Audience answers the question "To whom is this portfolio directed?" Audience refers to the person or persons for whom the portfolio is produced — that is, the primary reader or readers of the portfolio. Typically, portfolios are tailored to fit the requirements indicated by a particular audience, such as an instructor, an employer, or a certification board. Specific audiences are assumed in given contexts. Different audiences expect and look for different things. Identifying and understanding these requirements and expectations is part of the portfolio builder's initial challenge.

The following examples illustrate the relationships among elements — purpose, type, context, and audience — that constitute the portfolio orientation. If, for instance, the purpose is to provide a basis for evaluation in the context of a job search, a professional portfolio will be developed. The audience will be the individual, panel, or committee conducting the interview. A second use of portfolios with the purpose of providing a basis for evaluation is found in a college course. An assessment portfolio may be used to demonstrate what you have learned and can do in relation to the subject matter and skills specified in the course. The primary audience will be the instructor.

A CLOSER LOOK AT PURPOSE

Purpose is central to the portfolio process, a kind of guiding beacon. Every aspect of the portfolio project should clearly connect to the purpose. Wolf and Dietz (as cited in Bartell, Kaye, & Morin, 1998) point out that "the portfolio purpose is instrumental in shaping the form, content, and process of the portfolio" (p. 7). We find that there are three general purposes that portfolios serve. They are used to:

1. Facilitate and chart development
2. Provide a basis for evaluation
3. Highlight performance and capabilities

It is important to note that these purposes need not be mutually exclusive, although each can stand alone. Each purpose is valuable in and of itself. Any of the purposes may initially be the primary driving force behind the development of a portfolio. Portfolios are not one-size-fits-all documents, nor is a single portfolio intended to meet the needs of every audience. Instead, they are tailored to fit specific needs for specific purposes. If constructed with care, they are easily adapted. Adaptation may involve additions, deletions, reformulation, or reconfiguration of materials. With adaptation, however, a portfolio may serve several purposes over time and be used in different contexts. In all cases, as stand alone, single-purpose documents or as sequential-use documents, they must remain congruent with your philosophy, which is reflective of who you are. We think of portfolios as having the potential for being living documents that can develop and mature with their builders throughout their careers. Although we have seen very few references to this notion of multiple, sequential purposes in the literature, we have found it useful and applicable in a variety of adult and higher education settings. Here are a couple of examples of multiple, sequential purposes.

In a degree completion option in child development at our university, students create comprehensive program portfolios. Their portfolios are intended from the outset to accomplish two purposes: (a) to demonstrate professional competency in relation to National Association for the Education of Young Children (NAEYC) Standards for Programs over the course of a 43-unit program, and (b) to highlight performance and capabilities through integrated projects designed to improve practice. Each portfolio entry represents a significant activity or product that the students (full-time working professionals in early care and education settings) have developed and implemented at their work sites or in the professional community. Each portfolio entry embodies and illustrates their learning in multiple content areas (e.g., curriculum, working with diverse families, advocacy). The portfolio in its entirety provides a portrait of the students' holistic learning and accomplishments relative to the program curriculum. At the conclusion of the program, many students adapt their portfolios to a second purpose — to provide a basis for evaluation. The original portfolios often constitute the basis for professional portfolios, which they develop at a later date.

Another example of multiple, sequential purposes is seen in an option within the teaching credential program. Students first develop assessment portfolios that demonstrate their knowledge of, and ability to apply, state teaching standards in their practicum experience. The purpose of these portfolios at the outset is to facilitate and chart their development. In the context of the college course, the portfolios are required, but not graded. Students are counseled as to the future potential value and use of these portfolios as a tool in job seeking. At the end of the credential program, graduates often adapt their portfolios to this second purpose — which is evaluative — as an aid in interviewing for their first teaching positions. Later, as first-year teachers, they use these portfolios for a third purpose — to facilitate and chart their development — this time with their mentors. The portfolios serve as a foundation and directional tool to inform and individualize their continuing professional development. Their portfolios become vehicles for ongoing professional conversation.

Understanding purpose is central to understanding the portfolio. Purpose dictates the type of portfolio to be developed and, by association, indicates both context and audience. In the next section, we discuss purpose in relation to type, context, and audience.

RELATIONSHIPS: PURPOSE, TYPE, CONTEXT, AND AUDIENCE

In this section we discuss how all of these aspects of portfolio orientation — purpose, type, context, and audience — fit together, using purpose as the organizing element. We identify the type, context, and audience most commonly associated with each purpose. Table 3-1 below provides an overview of portfolio orientation.

TABLE 3-1
PORTFOLIO ORIENTATION OVERVIEW

Purpose	*Type*	*Context*	*Audience*
Facilitates and charts development	Developmental	Professional development Mentor/mentee relationships	Mentor, self
Highlights expertise	Showcase	Professional gatherings Exhibitions	Self, instructors, professional community
Provides a basis for evaluation	Assessment	Preservice teacher preparation Teacher evaluation (of those already practicing) Applying for national teacher certification	Instructors, certification board
	Professional	Job searches Preparation for promotion	Potential or current employers

PURPOSE AS IT APPLIES TO ALL TYPES OF PORTFOLIOS

Portfolios offer windows into the learning process and, in this way, serve a descriptive function. For many students, the emphasis of previous schooling was on acquiring knowledge, and on the knowledge itself. Little attention was paid to *how* a particular student learns, and how her value system and life experience influence *what* she learns. More recently, individuals' learning styles, strengths, challenges, and ways of knowing have been viewed as important factors in the learning process. Portfolios, in general, function as an excellent medium for examining and understanding one's process of growth and development, learning, and change. They provide valuable insights into how and what one learns, and they facilitate that learning.

Portfolios are intended to catalyze self-examination and transformation. They are personal explorations. By way of transformation, this portfolio type is intended to introduce the portfolio builders, or bring them, to a higher level of mindful practice. Langer (1997) describes this notion of mindfulness as having three characteristics: "the continuous creation of new categories; openness to new information, and an implicit awareness of more than one perspective" (p. 4). Mindfulness requires that you bring your habitual ways of doing into consciousness, and then closely examine them in light of new information and fresh perspectives. A portfolio acts, in part, as a journal in which you record and consider connections made between theory and practice.

PURPOSE 1: TO FACILITATE AND CHART DEVELOPMENT

Portfolios in which the primary purpose is to facilitate and chart development emphasize work in progress. They foster the development of knowledge, skills, and dispositions that will be employed in subsequent learning and practice contexts. These portfolios provide a mechanism for increasing self-assessment, reflection, observation, and other skills necessary for reflective professional practice. The builder is not alone in these endeavors. Mentors play an indispensable role — that of engaging the builders in collegial dialogue through which questions are raised, problems are explored, skills are refined, solutions are tested, results are examined, and emotions are expressed.

Developmental Portfolios Facilitate and Chart Development

The *type* of portfolio that facilitates and charts development is called *developmental*. Developmental portfolios are also called "learning" (Wolf & Dietz, 1998) and "professional development" (Dietz, 1995) portfolios. Developmental portfolios function as a means for documenting and charting growth in knowledge, skills, and dispositions over a specified period of time. The "specified period of time" can vary greatly. It can span an accelerated one-month course, a semester course, or a program. By their very nature, developmental portfolios provide a great deal of flexibility. Because they focus on the learning needs of the students, they can be individualized. The instructor or mentor determines their contents, often in dialogue with the student.

At our university, undergraduates in a degree completion option produce developmental portfolios at various points throughout the four semesters of the program. These portfolios document the learner's growing ability to formulate increasingly insightful and pertinent questions and master needed skills. They show progression in the organization of one's thinking and in its complexity. And they demonstrate gains in one's facility in identifying, locating, retrieving, organizing, and presenting data, and identifying and translating conceptual knowledge into practical applications.

Developmental portfolios give the builder room to acquire new knowledge, experiment, practice, analyze, and reflect on real-world tasks that have personal meaning. Successive drafts or reviews of tasks that show increasing understanding or proficiency over time are common to these portfolios. This content reflects the formative nature of developmental portfolios, wherein the builder and mentor systematically analyze progress and identify next steps toward a goal. Developmental portfolios focus on process and self-improvement.

Contexts in Which Developmental Portfolios Are Used

Developmental portfolios are commonly used in contexts in which the participants engage in dialogue meant to broaden and deepen understanding, and to stimulate reflection on practice. These contexts are generally geared toward engaging students in the practical application of knowledge and skills. Bartell and colleagues (1998) describe portfolios as providing a basis for collegial conversations "with a mentor, colleague, or 'critical friend'" (p. 131). In our work, we use developmental portfolios with two different groups. With final student teachers in a credential program, the portfolio focus is on making connections between standards and students' experiences in field placements. The portfolio gives the student a place to try on reflective habits of mind, apply skills, and examine practice. With practitioners in the degree completion program, the portfolio focus is on using knowledge in new ways, building specific skills and critical self-awareness, and informing ongoing practice. These practitioners often work with one another collaboratively as colleagues, sharing their ideas and drafts, with the goal of helping each other improve, and thus strengthening the work of all. Their efforts are reciprocal and mutually beneficial, and are guided by their mentor. Their mentor helps them establish appropriate benchmarks and timelines, and together they critique and improve portfolio entry ideas, plans, and finished products.

Audiences for the Developmental Portfolio

Audiences commonly associated with developmental portfolios include the self, instructors, mentors, and colleagues-as-mentors. Mentors expect and look for evidence of the portfolio builder's growth in several key areas. These include the following: self-assessment of knowledge, skills, and learning needs ("What do I know?"); inquiry ("What else do I need to know and how can I come to know it?"); reflection ("How do I know what I know and what does it all mean?"); and self-assessment of performance and professionalism ("How am I doing?").

PURPOSE 2: TO PROVIDE A BASIS FOR EVALUATION

Portfolios used for evaluation purposes provide a basis for judgment of one's performance and accomplishments against established external criteria. They document, for instance, the degree to which a student meets criteria in a course or program. A certain level of success is required before the student can continue in the program or graduate from it. The portfolio reflects the external criteria that are applied. The criteria are based on the standards one must address, such as those developed by the instructor or dictated by the institution, state, or professional association. Evaluation occurs to determine if, and the degree to which, the criteria have been satisfied.

The portfolio also serves as a threshold to future work. It demonstrates one's preparedness to assume positions beyond one's teacher preparation program or current job. The competencies in knowledge, skills, dispositions, and the accomplishments presented provide strong indications of what a school principal or other employer can expect in a candidate's future performance in relation to job expectations. Not only, then, do evaluation portfolios represent the degree to which external criteria have been met, but they also indicate whether given criteria are likely to be met in the future.

Assessment and Professional Portfolios Provided a Basis for Evaluation

Unlike the builder of the developmental portfolio, the builder of an evaluation portfolio does not influence the makeup of the standards, nor does she necessarily influence the performance criteria. These stand outside of the builder. There are two types portfolios used for evaluation purposes: *assessment* and *professional.*

Assessment portfolios have been part of professional schools (e.g., graphic design, architecture) for a very long time. Schools of education across the country and abroad have adopted portfolios, which are now widely used as tools to assess students' knowledge, skills, dispositions, and accomplishments against state, national, and professional association standards. They are also increasingly being used to assess teacher education programs by bodies such as the National Council for Accreditation of Teacher Education (NCATE). Assessment portfolios provide evidence of what students have learned in relation to specific external criteria, how they know what they know, and how they are able to apply what they know to achieve identified outcomes.

Professional portfolios are a second type used for evaluation purposes. They demonstrate one's potential fit and qualifications relative to employment or promotion criteria within a particular setting. They are tailored to emphasize the best of what one has to offer. They provide a point-in-time portrait of one's knowledge, skills, and dispositions, and they demonstrate the competence with which one can engage these in the work environment. They illuminate, through one's accomplishments, the benefits that the employer would gain by employing or advancing the candidate. Professional portfolios are also called "employment" (Wolf & Dietz, 1998) and "presentation" (Dietz, 1995) portfolios. Professional portfolios are increasingly used in the early care and education field as job-seeking and career advancement tools.

Contexts in Which Evaluation Portfolios Are Used

The most common contexts in which evaluation portfolios are used are in courses or programs and in employment settings. These portfolios include samples of one's best work from which others can determine how well the portfolio builder's skills, knowledge, and dispositions demonstrate competency, or fit the job qualifications, promotion criteria, or certification requirements. The preservice student asks, "How can I demonstrate my competence and readiness to assume a professional position?" The preemployment candidate asks, "How can I use what I've learned to meet the qualifications of this position?" The promotion candidate asks, "How can I prove my readiness to assume greater responsibilities?"

The following examples illustrate how we use these two types of evaluation portfolios. In the culminating experience for child development majors at our university, students complete an assessment portfolio. It is a comprehensive course portfolio in which they document their knowledge of child growth and development in infants, toddlers, and preschoolers using a variety of methods and theoretical frameworks. They demonstrate their skills in observation and analysis, curriculum planning and implementation, and assessment. They reveal their dispositions and growth through ongoing reflection. Through these assessment portfolios, students demonstrate their mastery in areas prescribed in a specific set of guidelines. Students show what they know and what they can do against the backdrop of expectations for knowledge and performance.

This second example of evaluation types illustrates one use of the professional portfolio. The teacher candidate, now a graduate of a teacher preparation program, brings her portfolio to her job interview with the principal of the school in which she would like to work. The principal asks her to describe how she will teach reading to second-graders. As she answers, she opens her portfolio to the curriculum section in which she has displayed photographs with captions detailing real in-classroom experiences with teaching reading. She uses the portfolio as a visual aid that makes her narrative come alive.

Audiences for Evaluation Portfolios: Assessment and Professional

Audiences commonly associated with assessment portfolios include instructors, field placement supervisors, and certification boards, such as the National Board for Professional Teaching Standards (NBPTS). For professional portfolios, audiences typically include potential employers and current employers. They may also include scholarship committees, internship evaluators, or admissions boards or committees.

These types of audiences look for and expect to see evidence of excellence and promise. Their evaluations often involve high stakes, since they result in determinations whether or not an individual passes the course, graduates from the program, or secures the job or promotion. They are also frequently competitive, wherein an individual is ranked in relation to others, or is compared against others vying for the same position.

PURPOSE 3: TO HIGHLIGHT PERFORMANCE AND CAPABILITIES

Portfolios whose purpose is to highlight the builders' performance and capabilities function differently than do all of the other types. They do not serve the same type of summative evaluation purpose as assessment or professional portfolios; they go far beyond the instructive purpose of developmental portfolios. Their focus, instead, is on showcasing builders' accomplishments, and highlighting professional capabilities and interests. Showcasing provides builders with an opportunity to advertise their know-how.

Showcase Portfolios Highlight Performance and Capabilities

The type of portfolio that highlights performance and capabilities is called the *showcase* portfolio. Builders use showcase portfolios as a medium through which they integrate and synthesize their learning to produce complex work products. Rather than demonstrating competence in a variety of discrete elements within a set of standards, as in assessment portfolios, builders of showcase portfolios articulate their learning through products of their design that simultaneously draw on and address multiple standards. The products are made public through their use in the builders' work settings, giving these portfolios an in-the-present, active orientation. They document major learning achieved across the curriculum and provide evidence of integration and application of new knowledge and enhanced skills that are shown to have improved the builders' current practice. These portfolios make available to colleagues in the wider professional community results of important work that the builders have done to improve the quality of existing early care and education programs. They answer the questions, "What am I doing in my current practice?" "How have I used what I've learned in this course or program to improve my practice?" "How am I sharing my work with others?" "What do I have to offer the field?"

Contexts in Which Showcase Portfolios Are Used

Showcase portfolios are primarily used in the contexts of exhibitions or presentations to a professional community. They may be used in settings where employers come to shop for prospective employees. We use this type of portfolio in the child development degree completion option at our university. At their exhibition celebration, program graduates display their showcase portfolios, which highlight their learning and accomplishments as evidenced by specific work products. They share these accomplishments and products with their peers, instructors, families, and with the larger early care and education community. In this context, showcase portfolios aid graduates, who are working professionals, and the program in achieving four goals:

1. To contribute to and foster best practice,
2. To engage in and promote reflective practice, collaboration, and lifelong learning,
3. To cultivate a professional culture that thrives on inquiry and dialogue, and
4. To provide leadership in the early care and education field.

Audiences for Showcase Portfolios

Audiences commonly associated with showcase portfolios include instructors, colleagues in the wider professional community, peers, family members, prospective employers, and others connected in official capacities with the program, such as deans and department heads. Like the audiences for evaluation portfolios, showcase audiences are looking for and expect to see evidence of excellence. They also, however, anticipate innovation — new ways of addressing old problems and fresh expressions of recurring themes.

A FINAL NOTE

Understanding purpose, type, context, and audience and their interaction is an important step in preparing to undertake the development of a portfolio. Having a clear orientation, led by certain knowledge of your portfolio's purpose, sets the direction for all of the work that follows.

Chapter 4

Philosophy: The Unifying Element of Portfolios

If you're not sure where you're going, you're liable to end up someplace else *and not even know it.*

—Robert Mager

YOUR EDUCATIONAL PHILOSOPHY

Who are you as a professional? How does your knowledge and experience shape your practice? What role has education played in your life? And why did you choose early care and education as your field and education as your profession? The answers to these questions inform your educational philosophy and, consequently, have tremendous influence on your day-to-day practice. Your philosophy is a personal clarification and articulation of your educational beliefs and values. You define yourself by it; your practice reflects it. Before we can discuss the details of your educational philosophy, though, we want to put *philosophy* in context.

PHILOSOPHY: A QUICK REFRESHER

Philosophy is a word that is frequently used in education but infrequently explained. We believe that, in order to effectively articulate an educational philosophy, two things are important. First, you must understand what a philosophy is. Second, you must know the basis — or roots — of your values and beliefs about education. To these ends, we have defined the general construct of philosophy, located it in the context of education, and provided a brief explanation of the philosophies that are most prevalent in early care and education.

PHILOSOPHY AS A CONSTRUCT

Philosophy, in the broad sense, is a system of conscious and unconscious assumptions about the nature of humankind and the meaning of life. It is what comprises one's worldview. Worldview is highly personal. It is neither right nor wrong but is based on personal experiences and observations, and on knowledge derived from others. It asks, and answers, fundamental questions that have had deep, personal meaning to human beings since the beginning of time.

Over the centuries, likeminded people constructed distinct ways to explain the nature of life and the universe. Although they posed the same questions within metaphysical, epistemological, and axiological contexts, they arrived at different answers. As a result, a variety of philosophies emerged. Some of the oldest include idealism, realism, pragmatism, and existentialism. Figure 4-1 below (adapted from Webb, Metha, & Jordan, 1992) identifies philosophical contexts through which questions are asked and answers are sought. The diagram also shows the basic questions associated with each context. These contexts include the metaphysical (pertaining to the nature of reality and the cosmos, the epistemological (addressing the nature of knowledge and knowing), and the axiological (concerned with the nature of ethics, values, and aesthetics). Although it is beyond the scope of this book to discuss Western civilization's great philosophies, suffice it to say that much of how contemporary society thinks about education is rooted in these systems of thought.

Contexts of Philosophy

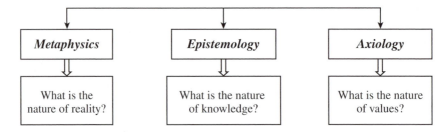

Figure 4-1.   Philosophical Contexts.

PHILOSOPHY IN THE CONTEXT OF EDUCATION

Just as humans have constructed different, and often conflicting, philosophies to answer the grand questions about life in general, educators have built different, and often conflicting, philosophies in response to questions specific to the nature, purpose, and value of education. In this section, we focus on the educational philosophies that are most likely to be encountered in early care and education settings. In earlier chapters, we discussed two of these: Constructivism and Behaviorism. In Table 4-1 we have summarized these along with two other prominent philosophies. We have connected each philosophy to the principles within the three philosophical contexts, to their educational aims, and to their implications for educational practice.

WHY GO TO THE TROUBLE
TO CONSIDER PHILOSOPHY?

To answer this question, look again at the definition of philosophy, this time, with education in mind:

> Philosophy is a system of conscious and unconscious assumptions about the nature of education. It is based on personal experiences and observations, and on knowledge derived from others. It asks, and answers, questions that are fundamentally important in education.

Fundamental questions for educators include: What is the aim of education? What is the nature of knowledge and knowing? Who should be educated? What is education's value to society?

Closely examining your personal experience, observations, and knowledge about education in light of these questions is a first step in uncovering the beliefs and values that motivate and direct your educational behavior. It enables you to determine "the principles that define [your] views about the learner, the teacher, and the [setting]" (Webb et al., 1992, p. 174). The answers to these questions help to establish your identity as an educator. While many educators subscribe to a particular philosophy, it is not uncommon for educators to assume a more eclectic perspective in which principles are drawn from multiple philosophies. Uncovering your beliefs and values about education brings you face-to-face with the principles that form your personal philosophy. Now it is time to begin building your own philosophy statement.

PHILOSOPHY STATEMENT: THE UNIFYING
ELEMENT OF PORTFOLIOS

Every portfolio must have a place from which to begin. We believe that a portfolio begins — and ultimately ends — with a carefully crafted philosophy statement. The portfolio process begins with an initial articulation of your philosophy. The statement is revised, further developed, and refined through

TABLE 4-1

SUMMARY OF EDUCATIONAL PHILOSOPHIES

	Metaphysics	Epistemology	Axiology	Aim of Education	Implications for Practice
Progressivism (Constructivism comes out of Progressivism.)	Reality is experience. It derives from interactions between the individual and his environment and changes over time.	Knowledge comes to be known through experimentation using the scientific method. Truth is never fully known.	What is ethically or morally good is judged on the basis of what works for the larger community. It is relative and situational.	To promote autonomy, problem solving, lifelong learning, and social responsibility	**Teacher:** Facilitator and guide. **Student:** Self-directed, intrinsically motivated, actively engaged with the environment and with others. **Practices:** Cooperative learning, problem setting and problem solving; open-ended activities, experimentation.
Existentialism	Perception is reality. Reality is determined by each individual. People have free will.	Knowledge is personal and comes through personal choices. The individual is responsible for his own knowledge.	Values are a matter of what one freely chooses and is, therefore, responsible for one's behaviors on the basis of those choices.	To recognize and accept personal responsibility. To acknowledge individuality. "March to one's own drum."	**Teacher:** Relates to each student as an individual, stresses individual responsibility and choice. **Student:** Chooses own means of expression, demonstrates personal responsibility, is at peace with own uniqueness. **Practice:** Individualizes instruction, open classroom with free choice.

Behaviorism	There is no such thing as free will. Individuals are products of their external environment.	External stimuli are the source of all knowledge. Learning is a response to external stimuli.	Values are environmentally formed.	To promote conformity to authority, passivity.	**Teacher:** Reinforces desirable behaviors using rewards. **Student:** Follows directions, engages in programmed learning. **Practices:** Skill-and-drill exercises, mastery of discrete bits of knowledge, use of worksheets, decontextualized learning.
Essentialism	The physical world is the basis for reality.	Knowledge is derived through application of the scientific method.	Natural and moral laws are absolute.	To produce competent and productive members of society. "Back-to basics."	**Teacher:** The center of the classroom — sets the moral standard, stays focused on the basics (eliminating anything considered nonessential), transmits knowledge. **Student:** Receives useful information as delivered by the teacher. **Practices:** Lecture on essential information, whole-group instruction on basics.

reflection-in-action (Schon, 1983) over the course of the portfolio process. The process ends with revisiting the statement to ensure that the practice represented in the portfolio is truly reflective of, and congruent with it. Ultimately, the philosophy statement unifies all elements within the portfolio. It is the statement of who you are as a professional and what principles guide your practice.

JUST WHAT IS A PHILOSOPHY STATEMENT?

A philosophy statement is a concise, written description of your beliefs and values specific to teaching and learning. It is a personal representation — or vision — of your ideal self and the ideal practice to which you aspire. The philosophy statement serves as a blueprint — guiding you, using the personally meaningful signs and symbols you determine — toward an image of your ideal teaching/learning self. As such, the philosophy statement is not something that can be proved or disproved. It is not right or wrong. The statement is used as a reference point against which you check to see if your practice matches your beliefs, and if the evidence collected accurately and authentically reflects your practice.

WHAT DOES A PHILOSOPHY STATEMENT DO AND WHY IS IT IMPORTANT?

The philosophy statement makes explicit, and publicly communicates, your philosophical point of view and theoretical groundings — the foundational ideas that are consistent with your larger worldview. It expresses the principles that guide your decision making. It also provides a foundation for congruence, a base from which to reflect on practice — past, present, and future — and against which to evaluate all actions and activities that eventually become part of the portfolio. The statement keeps the big picture in front of you, allowing you to consider how the various parts fit seamlessly into the whole. It is a tool for confirming the connection between beliefs and practice, thus preserving the integrity between beliefs and practice. It also provides a backdrop for self-evaluation and the establishment of realistic expectations and goals.

THE PHILOSOPHY–THEORY CONNECTION

The great world philosophies express the general assumptions and speculations human beings have about existence. Educational philosophies constitute the beliefs and values educators have about the nature and purpose of education. Theories, on the other hand, are sets of scientifically derived principles or ideas used to explain phenomena. Theories are used to support one's philosophy. Each professional educator has an obligation to know, and to be able to articulate, his or her philosophical and theoretical roots. Clear, strong, linkages between philosophy and theory ground the philosophy statement and give an educator professional credibility. It moves the statement beyond personal opinion and connects it something larger than oneself — the professional knowledge base.

DISPOSITIONS: GETTING INTO THE RIGHT FRAME OF MIND

We have described portfolios as representing knowledge, skills, dispositions, and accomplishments. Knowledge, skills, and accomplishments can be readily observed or tested. However, *dispositions* is a concept that is harder to pin down. We want to pause a moment here to define "disposition" as, like "philosophy," it is a term often used without explanation in education.

We have all known people who had the knowledge, skills and, perhaps, talents to accomplish great things but failed to do so because they lacked the will or the discipline. They just were not inclined — or disposed — to work very hard at something in which they might otherwise have excelled.

Katz (1995) defines "dispositions" as consistent and frequent patterns of behavior wherein the individual acts intentionally, or mindfully, in particular contexts and at particular times. These "ways of responding [are] more determined by characteristics internal to the actor than provoked by the environment" (p. 51). They constitute "habits of mind," rather than "mindless habits" (p. 57). In contrast to the notion of "habits of mind," Langer (1997) defines mindlessness as "entrapment in old categories; by automatic behavior that precludes attending to new signals; and by action that operates from a single perspective. Being mindless . . . is like being on automatic pilot . . ." (p. 4).

Considering your philosophy requires mindfulness — an intentional look at the things that move you, that shape your worldview. Therefore, it is worth a moment to assess your habits of mind in relation to teaching and learning in preparation for working on a philosophy statement.

Habits of mind — dispositions — that are useful in this process include flexibility of thought, intellectual curiosity, perseverance, risk taking, and critical reflection. We have identified these particular dispositions as important because beliefs and values are often fixed and unconscious, requiring conscious, concerted, and sustained effort to see them and state them clearly. This can be a demanding and time-consuming effort — one that is often more difficult than it appears on the surface. We find that in asking students to critically examine their "habitual ways of thinking and acting" (Brookfield, 1987, pp. 15–16), some students experience anxiety, uncertainty, defensiveness, and even anger. Emotional responses such as these are not unusual and are often part of the (holistic) Constructivist process.

We offer a few short anecdotes to illustrate the importance of reevaluating our habitual practices and making conscious decisions about what we really believe and why we believe it. The first is a story about a grown woman whose mother had come for a visit:

> The mother was sitting in the kitchen while her daughter prepared dinner. The daughter cut off both ends of the roast before putting it into the roasting pan. Her mother watched, and then chuckled. The daughter asked what had amused her. In response, her mother asked, "Why did you cut off the ends like that?" Her daughter thought for a moment, and then replied, "When I was growing up, that's what I always saw you do." The mother chuckled again, and explained that she had cut off the ends of roasts because her roasting pan was too small for whole roasts to fit.

The moral of the story is that the daughter had continued practicing a habit that made no sense in the current context, but she had never stopped to question the practice.

A second story comes from a recent child development class. Students were studying play in the context of the preschool playground, particularly as it relates to rough-and-tumble play. The literature drew sharp distinctions between aggressive play and aggression in children. Students conducted focused observations of both in their programs over a period of weeks, then discussed their observations in light of their reading. In a reflection at the conclusion of this learning sequence, one student wrote:

> In every program I have ever worked in, the children have never been allowed to play in a rough and tumble way. At the least, it's considered rowdy behavior that is unnecessary. At the worst, it's considered aggression and kind of violent. I never questioned these ideas. I just know that everybody seems to agree that it's bad for children. After studying rough and tumble play — and really looking at the children — I realize that it has value, it's normal, and that it is really different from a play problem where a child uses aggression to get his way or take out frustration. I just never thought about it before. This experience has led to a discussion among our whole staff about play — our understanding of it and our rules about it. We are planning a staff training on it and we are talking about having it as the topic of our spring parent night.

These stories illustrate how people frequently continue doing things because, in their experience, that is how they observed them done or were told they must be done. They had never questioned why. Each of us has a professional obligation to consciously make informed decisions about best practices, and to choose from multiple approaches those that are congruent with one's own beliefs (Schon, 1983).

PHILOSOPHY STATEMENT ESSENTIALS

Over the years we have developed guidelines to assist early care and education students and practitioners in developing philosophy statements. The guidelines for content that we delineate here meet our vision of what a philosophy statement is and what it should contain. Philosophy statements should summarize the portfolio builder's philosophical and theoretical foundations, and they should address how teaching and learning practices are expressed in the context of those foundational beliefs. Table 4-2 summarizes the components of a philosophy statement. The order in which they are addressed and presented are the prerogative of each writer.

TABLE 4-2

COMPONENTS OF A PHILOSOPHY STATEMENT

1. Philosophical Foundation: The nature, aim/s, and value of education.
2. Theoretical Foundation: The theories and/or research that ground the philosophy.
3. Learning: The source of motivation for learning, and how people learn.
4. Roles and Relationships: The teacher's and student's roles in learning. The nature of the teacher–student relationship. The relationship between the environment and learning. The nature of your relationship with others: colleagues, parents, the community.

As a way to get started, we have briefly explained each component and identified some questions that you might consider in developing a philosophy statement. These are not the only questions; there may be others that occur to you as you proceed. We have also included excerpts from students' philosophy statements that illustrate the components.

Philosophical Foundation: The Nature, Aim, and Value of Education

Keep in mind that this component deals with the nature of reality, knowledge, and values. It is the philosophical underpinning of the statement. It answers such questions as, "What is early care and education about?" "Where does knowledge come from?" "Is it constructed or is it transmitted?" "Why does early care and education exist?" "What does it hope to achieve and for whom?" "What value is it to society?"

Excerpts from students' statements:

Another responsibility of educators is to help students become socialized, competent, and educated.

An integral part of education is to help students become lifelong learners.

Theoretical Foundation: The Theories and/or Research that Ground the Philosophy

In model statements, clear connections are drawn between philosophical and theoretical foundations. If, for instance, you believe that children learn by doing, then the sources of theoretical support would most likely be the theories of Progressivists such as Dewey, and Constructivists such as Piaget and Vygotsky. Questions that assist in sorting out the philosophical/theoretical connections might include, "What in the early care and education knowledge base explains what you believe?" "With what research are you familiar that explains your beliefs?"

Excerpts from students' statements:

> Consistent with Piaget's theory of cognitive development, I believe that infants and toddlers learn about the world through their senses and by interacting with their environment.

> I believe that first, children's needs must be sensitively and consistently met so that they learn to trust their caregivers and develop secure attachments to them. I base this belief on both Erikson's psychosocial theory of human development and Maslow's hierarchy of needs.

Learning: The Source/s of Motivation for Learning and How People Learn

This component is at the heart of your philosophy statement. It addresses what compels people to learn and how knowledge comes to be known. It answers the questions, "*Why* do people learn? For instance, do you believe that children are basically motivated to learn due to intrinsic desires and natural curiosity? Or, instead, do you believe that learning is motivated by external forces? What do you believe about *how* people, in general, learn? Do you believe that learning is an active or a passive process on the part of the learner? Does knowledge come from one's interactions with the world, or as a result of one person transmitting knowledge to another?"

Excerpts from students' statements:

> Children are born with a natural curiosity to experiment with, explore, and investigate their environment.

> Because most children are intrinsically motivated, they will want to learn as much about themselves and their environment as they can.

Roles: The Teacher's and Student's Roles in Learning. The Nature of the Teacher–Student Relationship. The Relationship Between the Environment and Learning. The Nature of Your Relationships with Others: Colleagues, Parents, the Community.

How you see the teacher's role should be congruent with your beliefs about the source of motivation for learning and about how you believe learning occurs. If, for instance, you believe that students are active learners, and that learning is driven by natural curiosity, then the teacher's role could be to facilitate, coach, foster, and encourage. If you believe that students are passive learners who learn best when the learning is transmitted and reinforced by others, then the teacher's role could be to lecture, reward, praise, dictate. What do you believe the teacher's role is in relationship to students' learning?

Excerpts from students' statements:

> The teacher should initiate learning by creating interest, sparking curiosity, and guiding the learning process.

> The role of the teacher is to respect the children, to meet their needs and to establish a safe, stimulating environment which invites children to explore. Many different experiences should be provided to promote growth in every area of children's development, while the teacher stays close by to encourage the children's explorations, help them recognize boundaries and celebrate the joy of their discoveries.

Just as your view of the teacher's role should be congruent with your beliefs about the source of motivation for learning and what you believe about how learning occurs, so must the student's role be congruent. Burk and Dunn (1996) suggest that "Constructivists view autonomy as the aim of education" (p. 11). If you subscribe to this view, then the student's role could include active engagement on his own behalf, questioning authority and setting and solving problems.

Excerpts from students' statements:

> In the classroom, it is the responsibility of the students to participate in creating the classroom rules and therefore maintain their behavior.

> The role of the children is to explore and interact with their surroundings, to make choices based on their interests, and to master their bodies while learning to stay within boundaries.

Different philosophies ascribe different roles to the environment and its place in learning. What part do you believe the environment plays in learning? Is it the source of learning, as the Behaviorists believe? Does it support and facilitate learning, as the Constructivists believe?

Excerpts from students' statements:

> I believe that the environment should be safe, stimulating, and should invite children to explore.

> The environment plays an important part in children's learning. It supports their curiosity and it reflects their interests.

How do you see yourself in relation to others in the learning environment? Are you a partner with parents in children's learning? Do you see the community as an integral part of the learning environment, or as something separate from and beyond the scope of the classroom? Do you view colleagues as supports, collaborators, resources? Do you value teamwork, or do you prefer more solitary enterprise? Considering how you conceive of the learning environment and its role in children's learning is essential.

Excerpts from students' statements:

> I believe that the neighborhood is an extension of the classroom and offers many opportunities to enrich the curriculum.

> Collaboration and teamwork between parents and the school are essential to effective education for children. I am committed to meaningful parent and community involvement in my classroom.

Many of the examples above illustrate discrete parts of components of a philosophy statement in order to make the meaning of each clear. Several excerpts address more than one aspect of a component or more than one component. Keep in mind that your goal is ultimately to integrate all of the components, in total, into a seamless statement. We have included two sample statements that illustrate this integration. Although their authors teach at different levels, each statement incorporates the four elements: philosophical foundation, theoretical foundation, learning motivation and process, and the roles and relationships in learning.

Laurel's Philosophy Statement (Preservice, Elementary School)

> I believe that all children have a natural curiosity and the ability to learn. As a teacher it is my job to foster this curiosity through education of the whole child, in mind, body and spirit. Therefore, the environment we provide should be one that encourages this natural curiosity. If done so, children will exercise their abilities with great personal success.

> As a teacher, it is my job to make sure the environment is appropriate for all learners and to help children make meaningful connections. It is my job to find a way to bring out the individual talents that exists inside each child so that each one becomes a lifelong learner, fulfills his or her potential, and becomes a contributing member of our society.

Children learn when curriculum is meaningful. Children learn by doing. They achieve understanding by exploring and experimenting with their own ideas. This can be achieved by a classroom environment that uses many hands-on and project based activities.

I believe that instruction must be differentiated so that each child can use his or her own special "intelligence" and achieve success. I will be sensitive to the many different skills, preferences, and inclinations of different children, what one well-known researcher, Gardner, calls "intelligences," because I know that children learn in many different ways.

Based on the work of a second researcher, Maslow, I feel it is my job to make sure children are safe in my classroom, both physically and emotionally. In this way children will be open to taking risks. It is the job of the student to be an active learner, a risk taker, and a sharing, cooperating member of the classroom community.

My classroom will be child-centered with children's artwork displayed on the walls. Children will work in cooperative groups. Students will be engaged as a result of using developmentally appropriate curriculum. It is my goal to have students truly value learning. If I can do that, I will have given them the tools for success and I will have pointed them in the right direction.

Krishna's Philosophy Statement (Preschool)

My experience in working with children and families, along with my education on how children develop, has enabled me to construct a strong philosophy. It is based on my beliefs of how children learn best. Vygotsky has stated that with the guidance of a sensitive caregiver, who guides the transition from assisted performance to independent achievement, a child gains the sense that "I can." My goal is to facilitate each individual child's learning by challenging him or her at the appropriate level. My belief system is congruent with the point of view that a responsibility of educators is to help students become socialized, competent, and educated.

Children come into the world like a sponge, taking in everything. As they grow, their inborn desire to learn is heightened. So, by providing each child with meaningful, appropriate opportunities to build on their previous experiences and schemas, learning takes place. I believe that through using their senses and with hands-on, active play in a fun, open atmosphere, children are able to gain a better understanding of themselves and their work. Through play they are able to master skills, which helps build their positive self-concept.

My role as an educator of young children is to provide a supportive and safe environment from which to explore, to enable each child the opportunity to reach their full potential. I feel that by establishing a strong relationship with the children and their families, I am better equipped to give each child what he or she needs and wants, and also demonstrate my respect for the wishes of the family. By modeling respect, patience, and love for each individual person (child or adult), I am providing a base from which my relationships stem and my lessons begin. The children are then able to actively engage in their environment through materials and interactions with others and to make choices that develop who they are. I believe that the environment should be stimulating, culturally sensitive, full of positive messages, and provide open-ended experiences and opportunities to problem-solve and wonder.

All my life I've felt a deep desire to help others. As an adult I've decided to dedicate my life to creating our future generation. My goal is to guide each child so that, with a deep sense of "I can," he or she will go out and do. I truly believe in the power of positive guidance and acceptance for all the world's creatures. I plan to provide a healthy and positive first experience in the lives of children from all walks of life. This is my passion, my calling, to the world of children.

A FINAL NOTE

Philosophy statements are born from close self-examination of those things that silently direct and guide an educator's actions. Clarifying your philosophy frees you to make informed, consistent choices in your practice. By communicating your philosophy, you tell others what they can expect from you, and it serves as a reminder to you of your vision of ideal practice and ideal self.

Chapter 5

Reflection: The Defining Feature of Portfolios

Learning without thought is labor lost; thought without learning is perilous.

—Confucius

WHY REFLECTION IS THE DEFINING
FEATURE OF PORTFOLIOS

We characterize reflection as the defining feature of portfolios because it is the mental process through which human beings convert experience into personal knowledge. It is reflection that distinguishes portfolios from scrapbooks or other kinds of collections. Reflections form a continuous thread that runs through the portfolio, tying artifacts to learning, and providing evidence of growth and change over time.

Reflection serves several important purposes. It helps you:

1. Bring experience and knowledge together to produce new learning that is personally meaningful
2. Connect theory to practice
3. Strengthen a critical reflection disposition
4. Gain insight into your learning and personal/professional development
5. Manage your emotions throughout the learning process

Reflection is a bridge between the cognitive and emotional states. It is a useful mechanism for examining the emotional impact of cognitively oriented content. As Mezirow (1991) explains, "Reflection is the central dynamic involved in problem solving, problem posing, and transformation of meaning schemes and meaning perspectives" (p. 116).

PREREQUISITES FOR REFLECTION

Reflection, like *philosophy*, is a word that is used more and more in education and other professional settings, but is too often left undefined and uncontextualized. Students and practitioners alike are asked to do more of it, but often have only a vague notion of what it is. We identify reflection as central to, and inextricable from, the portfolio process. As such, we think it is important for readers to understand how we interpret and contextualize reflection. To that end, we have addressed reflection from several vantage points: as a disposition, as a human capability, and as a cognitive skill that has application in, and is necessary to, professional practice.

In the previous chapter, we identified a number of dispositions (ways in which a person is inclined to behave) that we consider key to the portfolio process. Being critically reflective is one of these dispositions. In addition to being a disposition, we also see reflection as a human capability — that is, as a universal human potential. The capacity to reflect is a characteristic unique to human beings. It is one of the things that distinguishes humans from all other creatures. Even so, some people do not develop the capacity; it is not automatic. Many who do develop it use it circumstantially and to greater or lesser degrees in different areas of their lives.

Developing the capability for critical reflection requires higher order thinking skills, conscious engagement, and sustained effort. Four aspects of thinking (higher order skills) make reflection possible. The first of these is abstract thinking: a mental process whereby concepts that cannot be experienced directly through the senses can be understood, such as friendship and trust. The second is complex thinking: the ability to perceive multiple aspects or multiple levels of a problem or situation at the same time. The third is metacognition: awareness, not just of a problem or situation, but of one's thinking about one's thoughts on a problem or situation. It is thinking about thinking. The fourth is pragmatism: the ability to adapt logical thinking to the practical constraints of real-life situations and manage the ambiguity that often accompanies them (Arnett, 2004). These cognitive abilities usually begin to emerge in early adolescence. They develop over time and are enhanced through use, combined with modeling, mentoring, and instruction.

REFLECTION IN PRACTICE

We have briefly described reflection as a capability that humans possess, a disposition that some acquire, and a cognitive skill enabled by higher order thinking. Now we are going to talk about it as an essential professional practice.

Anthony Clark (as reported in Lyons, 1998) describes reflection as "thematic constructions of meaning taking place over time and drawn from multiple experiences" (p. 106). Clark's use of the phrase "thematic constructions of meaning" is instructive, in that it provokes an image of contemplating related behaviors to form a picture of how one habitually behaves in certain circumstances. For instance, how might a teacher think about and understand her interactions with parents generally? What does her examination of her behaviors with, or attitudes about, parents reveal to her about herself? How does she interpret her experiences with parents? What new information does she have that might influence her usual behaviors or ways of dealing with parents?

Clark goes on to say that, ". . . reflection ought to be considered as a drawing together of long strands of connections, the weaving together of experiences, theory, and practices into meaning for the individual . . . a kind of construction of knowledge . . ." (Lyons, 1998, p. 106). Here, he captures an important essence of reflection: the making of contextual meaning out of one's experience. Experience in this sense is the combination of one's prior knowledge, day-to-day experiences (past and present), and new knowledge. Learning, in large part, can be thought of as experience that has been reflected on. As Posner (2005) notes, "We do not actually learn from experience as much as we learn from reflecting on experience" (p. 21). We agree with both Clark and Posner. We define critical reflection as:

> the practice of intentionally bringing into conscious awareness one's motivations, thoughts, beliefs, questions, assumptions, feelings, attitudes, desires, and expectations for the purpose of gaining insightful understanding as to their meaning, their connections to what is personally known, and in light of new experiences and information. Reflection makes possible the insights necessary to learn from experience and alter habitual behaviors.

As the definition indicates, intentionality, or purposefulness, is an aspect of reflection. Without purpose, reflection is hollow — perhaps just random mental wanderings. We reflect on our actions and the actions of others with the intention of uncovering our motives, assumptions, beliefs, and the like, so that we may gain deeper understanding and make sense of things — to fit them into, or build new, constructs.

Behavior stems from one's motivations, thoughts, beliefs, questions, assumptions, feelings, attitudes, desires, and expectations. Reflection is a tool for the analysis of our observations and actions, their consequences, and their implications. Reflection aids us in imagining alternative ways of acting. It is a mechanism by which we can challenge ourselves to ask critical, and sometimes, life-changing questions. Reflection also allows us to go beyond ourselves — to challenge prevailing social, political, cultural, and professional beliefs and practices (Brookfield, 1995). Reflection is a tool for personal change. It is also a tool for social change.

REFLECTION AND LEARNING FRAMES

For purposes of portfolios, reflection is particularly well applied to three key learning frames. The approach you take to your written reflections may vary according to the learning frame that best applies. The learning frames include:

1. Experiences you have as an observer of self and others
2. Experiences you have as a critical reader of the professional literature
3. Experiences you have as an implementer of activities

Experiences You Have as an Observer of Self and Others

This frame is relationship oriented. The experiences you have as an observer of self and others encompass intrapersonal and interpersonal interactions. Intrapersonal interactions include observations you make of, and conversations you have with, yourself on matters of importance to you. Interpersonal interactions are those that include observations you make of, and with, others, such as those between yourself and a parent, between yourself and a child or group of children, between two children, between a child and teacher, or within a group of children. This frame concentrates on the qualities and content of relationships within the context of events.

Experiences You Have as a Critical Reader of the Professional Literature

Part of becoming a professional is learning to engage the literature rather than simply being a consumer of it. This learning frame focuses on both the rigor with which you explore the professional literature, and the disposition you bring to your reading of it. So often students have been taught to read for key points, memorize the key points, and produce them in some fashion on an exam. This approach strips reading of its meaning and value. Engaging the literature — reading critically — requires adopting an inquiring frame of mind. The critical reader asks questions such as, "What is the author really saying, and from what perspective?" "What does this mean to me?" "How is this important?" "How does this relate to my experience and/or prior knowledge?" "How does this fit with what I believe?" "How can I use this information?" "What questions does this raise for me?" "What else do I want to know about this?"

Experiences You Have as an Implementer of Activities

In producing artifacts for your portfolio, you will most likely conduct activities in conjunction with others — children and adults. This experience frame encompasses the experiences you have while conducting those activities. It focuses on the processes and products associated with your activities. For instance, this frame addresses issues related to the success, failure, challenges, strong and weak points, outcomes, and benefits of the activities as they apply to the criteria you are attempting to satisfy.

Experience frames are not mutually exclusive. A given experience may have aspects of two, or all three. In writing a reflection, consider the criterion you are addressing and what you are trying to convey. This will suggest the frame to which you may want to direct your primary attention.

Understanding what reflection can mean for you as a professional is the first step in making it a regular feature of your practice. Yet, knowing its importance and value can still leave you wondering how to go about it. In the next section, we discuss the components of reflection and offer several tools to assist you in structuring your written reflections.

BECOMING ACCOMPLISHED
IN WRITTEN REFLECTION

As with any skill, written reflection lies on a continuum, from developing to accomplished (Figure 5-1). And, as with any skill, becoming accomplished at it requires practice. Fink (2003) states that reflective writing, "when viewed as a process and when done properly, has a unique ability to develop the interior life of the writer. . . . [It] focuses on the writer's learning experience itself and attempts to identify the significance and meaning of a given learning experience, primarily for the writer" (pp. 116–117). The act of reflective writing, in a sense, forces the writer to examine, clarify, and crystallize thoughts and ideas that might otherwise be floating around the mind in disconnected fragments.

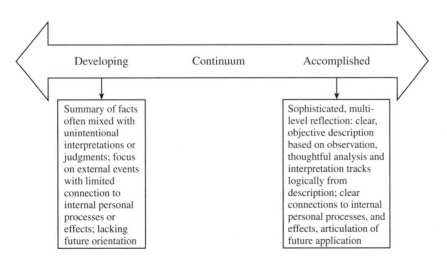

Figure 5-1. Reflection Continuum.

The process involved in reflection has four steps (Figure 5-2). Each step plays an important role in your learning and self-actualization. As you prepare to write each reflection, consider the experience on which you are reflecting in the context of the most salient learning frame, and focus on it through each step in the reflection process. The steps in the reflection process include:

1. Observation and description
2. Analysis and interpretation
3. Insights and implications
4. Projections and planning

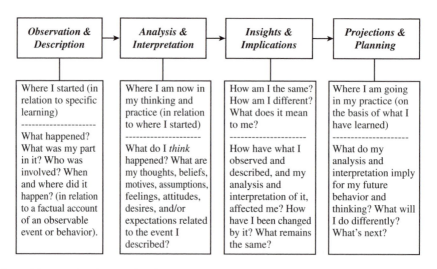

Figure 5-2. Four-Step Process of Reflection.

Description and Observation

Observation is at the heart of reflection. Your observations, of yourself and others in the context of your practice, form the basis of the descriptions on which you base your written reflections. When reflecting on your state of knowledge, skill, or disposition in relation to new knowledge or experience, you will want to describe where you were — in knowing and feeling — prior to that new exposure.

Even without being aware of it, you are constantly observing what goes on around you and trying to make sense of it. Human beings seek and order patterns in their physical and emotional environments, and try to fit them into existing patterns. Some of the observations you make will stand out for you. They will intrigue you, bother you, delight you, or concern you. They will fit your existing patterns, or they will violate them. The experiences that stand out for you are the ones to write about, because these are the ones that probably have meaning for you on some level. If you are unable to jot down notes on the spot (a running record), make notes as soon after the event as possible (an anecdotal record). Our minds lose track of details very quickly. Flesh out the details at your earliest opportunity in order to capture the most complete and accurate account. This stage of the process can take as little as a few minutes each day.

Descriptions of an observable event embody the same qualities as any good observation done for educational purposes. They are factual, objective, and concise. Curtis and Carter (2000) identify five qualities of a good observation:

1. Objectivity (seeing without judging, as though you were a camera lens)
2. Directness (recording direct quotes whenever possible)
3. Specificity (specific details: who was involved, when and where the action took place, your involvement in the event, and what actually happened)
4. Completeness (the story with a beginning, a middle, and an end, however brief)
5. Mood (the social and emotional details without interpretation: tone of voice, body language, facial expressions, hand gestures)

Descriptions do not include the assignation of motive, emotion, intentions, capabilities, or traits, even if they are your own. This first step in the process asks that you temporarily set aside your analysis (what you think was going on), interpretation (why you think it was going on), and judgment (whether you think it was right or wrong).

Those who are new to reflective writing often mistake description for reflection. This is why initial attempts at reflection often resemble summaries of facts or book reports, sometimes with unintentional interpretation and judgment mixed in. Keep in mind that the function of description in reflective writing is to establish the context of the event and to provide adequate detail that sets the stage for the analysis, interpretation, projection, and planning that follow.

Analysis and Interpretation

Analysis and interpretation involve careful examination of the motivations, thoughts, beliefs, questions, assumptions, feelings, attitudes, desires, and expectations that guide your thinking and behavior. Through analysis and interpretation, you consciously examine the "whys" behind your actions and the genesis of your thoughts and beliefs. The incidents or experiences you describe in a reflection may be representative of your habitual ways of thinking and acting in similar circumstances. Explore possible connections between your current and past actions and ideas. Carefully consider how what you have observed connects to, and is directed by, your motives, and so on. This is where insight comes from. Be thoughtful about how your experiences align with the theories you hold or with theories with which you have become newly acquainted. Bridging theory and practice is a challenge that this process can facilitate. Examine the impact of your observations on your personal beliefs and behaviors. This step can open the door to personal and professional transformation.

Making sense of an experience and coming to understand its impact do not always happen quickly. The sifting and sorting process can take a little time. Having some distance from an event provides the mental breathing space the mind needs to process the experience. We encourage students to set aside time at the end of each week to review their descriptions, check in on their mental wanderings, and write their reflections.

Insights and Implications

What have you learned from a given experience about yourself, about your practice, and about others? What has become clearer to you? The insight born of reflection offers a window into everyday experiences that are easily taken for granted. The familiar is often the overlooked. Yet, your careful, thoughtful appraisal of it can shed light on the truths that lie within.

No one operates in a vacuum. Your actions affect not only you, but also others around you. They can have a ripple effect – sometimes having an impact on people whom you have not met. Think about the outcomes and implications of your actions and observations. Consider the results of what you do on yourself and on those immediately affected by your actions. Anticipate the effects on those who may experience the consequences of your actions at a later time (e.g., the children who will be in your program next year who will benefit from a policy decision you make today). Insight fuels change.

Projection and Planning

How can the conclusions you draw be used to improve your practice now and in the future? Examine the insights you have gained in light of your philosophy statement and your current practices. Consider what your reflection has taught you and frame it against the vision you have of your ideal self and your ideal practice. What will you change? What has been validated? Contemplate the meaning of specific learning experiences in relation to the criteria to which you are being held. Use your insights to consider how what you have learned has changed you and what that may mean to your future. Determine the relevance and implications of your learning with regard to future action. In projection and planning, you answer the questions "So what (that I've learned this)?" and "Now what (do I do with it)?" This step moves you to action.

If you are new to writing reflectively, or to the steps we have discussed above, you might wonder how it all looks in a real reflection. In the next section, we have dissected a reflection to show you how one student incorporated and integrated the four steps.

ANATOMY OF A REFLECTION

You might look at the steps in the reflection process discussed above and wonder how you can cover all of those steps and still have time in your day for anything else! Reflective writing does take time and effort. However, written reflections do not have to be exhaustive tomes. They can be relatively brief pieces and still be effective. Manny's reflection (Figure 5-3) is one such example. We have pointed out where and how the steps of reflection were used (description, analysis, and interpretation; insights and implications; and projection and planning).

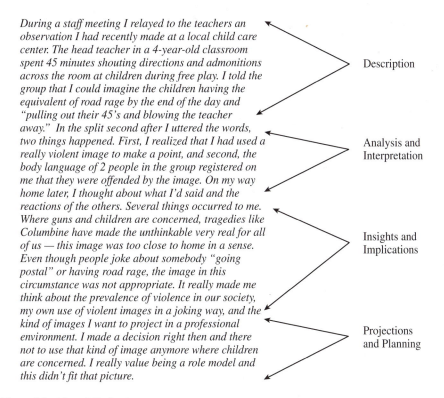

During a staff meeting I relayed to the teachers an observation I had recently made at a local child care center. The head teacher in a 4-year-old classroom spent 45 minutes shouting directions and admonitions across the room at children during free play. I told the group that I could imagine the children having the equivalent of road rage by the end of the day and "pulling out their 45's and blowing the teacher away." In the split second after I uttered the words, two things happened. First, I realized that I had used a really violent image to make a point, and second, the body language of 2 people in the group registered on me that they were offended by the image. On my way home later, I thought about what I'd said and the reactions of the others. Several things occurred to me. Where guns and children are concerned, tragedies like Columbine have made the unthinkable very real for all of us — this image was too close to home in a sense. Even though people joke about somebody "going postal" or having road rage, the image in this circumstance was not appropriate. It really made me think about the prevalence of violence in our society, my own use of violent images in a joking way, and the kind of images I want to project in a professional environment. I made a decision right then and there not to use that kind of image anymore where children are concerned. I really value being a role model and this didn't fit that picture.

Description

Analysis and Interpretation

Insights and Implications

Projections and Planning

Figure 5-3. Manny's Reflections.

TOOLS FOR WRITTEN REFLECTION

We have devised several tools to help students structure their reflections. The first tool has two parts: an Observation Log (Figure 5-4), and an Observation Follow-Up (Figure 5-5). The Observation Log includes columns for the description of the event, interpretation, and judgment — a physical reminder to discriminate among these three mental functions. Each section contains prompts and hints to assist the observer with the observation task. The log can be used for on-the-spot observations (running records) or for recording events after the fact (anecdotal records).

The Observation Follow-Up assists students with the sorting out of the analysis and interpret, insights and implications, and projection and planning aspects of the reflection. It also includes prompts to help students focus on what is most pertinent in each area.

OBSERVATION LOG#_____

Context: _____   **Date:**

Specify Learning Frame: Relationship or Activity — Describe
_____

Who was involved? (Use first names only.)
_____

When and where did it happen?
_____

Description	Interpretation	Judgment
What happened? What was my part in it? *Include complete sequence, be objective, specific, direct, indicate mood (facial expressions, body language, hand gestures – without interpretation).*	What do I think happened? What are my thoughts, beliefs, motivations, questions, assumptions, feelings attitudes, desires, and/or expectations related to this event?	What value have I associated with this event or the people involved? What capabilities or traits have I associated with them?
Sample descriptive words: hurried, squatted, gingerly, screeched, tossed, grabbed, pushed, firmly, roughly, busily, struggled; *any word that describes an action that videotape could covey.*	**Sample interpretive words:** seems, thinks, angry, appears, wants, likes, believes, meant to, understands, feels, it looks like, sad, on purpose, intentionally; *any word that indicates a motive, emotion, or intention.*	**Sample judgment words:** wrong, right, good, bad, nice, mean, honest, smart, dumb, pretty, trustworthy, spoiled; *any word that places a value on an action or person or assigns a trait or capability.*

Figure 5-4. Observation Log.

OBSERVATION FOLLOW-UP (Log # _____)		Date:
Analysis and Interpretation How has what I observed and described, and my analysis and interpretation of it, affected me? How have I been changed by it? What remains the same? What biases have I noticed? What is the source of my feelings about this event?	**Insights and Implications** What have I learned about myself? What has this made me question? What has it validated? How am I the same or different? What do my analysis and interpretation imply for my future behavior and thinking?	**Projection and Planning** What will I do differently? What will remain the same? Where am I going in my practice as a result of what I've learned?

Figure 5-5. Observation Follow-Up.

We encourage students to use the Observation Log and Observation Follow-Up on at least a weekly basis, or more often as events of note arise. When used consistently over a period of time, these two documents, used in tandem, constitute a field journal. The field journal can then serve as an excellent tool for longer-term or more global reflection.

In addition to the Observation Log and Observation Follow-Up, we provide students with a rubric for assessing their reflections (Table 5-1). The rubric is the scoring guide, or criteria, against which the reflections are assessed.

Another tool we have found helpful to students in writing their reflections is "Where I started — Where I am — What's next?" This set of prompts is often used when helping students engage the professional literature, and make sense of it in their individual contexts — the second learning frame. It is also affective when used to reflect on the implementation of an activity — the third learning frame. The example below illustrates the third learning frame. An intern in a teacher education program wrote it. She was reflecting on her efforts at "understanding and organizing subject matter for student learning," a content area in the state credentialing standards.

Zhling's Reflection

Where I Started . . .

As a novice teacher the biggest challenge for me was to make curriculum comprehensible to my special education students. Although I was comfortable with the subject matter, making it connect to the student was difficult. I learned that social needs are just as important and needing to be taught as are academics. I learned by trial and error in organizing curriculum and using teaching strategies. I was limited to resources that I could pull from. I didn't have a lot of supplementary materials at hand.

Where I Am . . .

I am now in a position where I can make connections from my past experiences as a teacher to help me in present situations. I've formed good relationships with my students and have learned to allow their needs to drive my instruction. I allow my students to develop as critical thinkers by presenting them with reasoning practice. I've learned that when enthusiasm is there on the part of the teacher, the students are more able to receive the lesson. My planning includes interrelating subjects to make learning meaningful and supportive.

TABLE 5-1

REFLECTION RUBRIC

	Developing	*Competent*	*Exemplary*
Observation and Description	May not include all parts. Language is not descriptive. Confuses interpretation and judgment with description.	Includes all parts, but with only some rich description. Mixes in some interpretation or judgment.	Employs all parts (complete, objective, direct, specific, mood) to tell the story. Uses rich, descriptive language. No interpretation or judgment.
Analysis and Interpretation	Little evidence of exploration and clarification of thoughts, beliefs, motives, assumptions, feelings, attitudes, desires, and/or expectations. Little evidence of examination of their meaning.	Shows some evidence of exploration and clarification of thoughts, beliefs, motives, assumptions, feelings, attitudes, desires, and/or expectations. Some examination of their meaning.	Explores and clarifies thoughts, beliefs, motives, assumptions, feelings, attitudes, desires, and/or expectations related to the event. Examines what these mean on personal and professional levels.
Insights and Implications	Little insight into self. Little if any reference to change that has taken place, what remains the same, how experiences have affected him/her. Little indication of awareness of implications as to how experiences will affect future.	Some insight into self. Indicates change that has taken place, what remains the same, how experiences have affected him/her. Indicates implications with some reference to how experiences will affect future.	Demonstrates excellent insight into self. Indicates change that has taken place, what remains the same, how experiences have affected him/her. Explains implications of experience for future.
Projections and Planning	Little if any evidence of projection based on experience. Scant evidence of planning for future actions in relation to the learning gained from the experience.	Some projection based on experience. Some evidence of planning for future actions in relation to the learning gained from the experience.	Clear projections into future in reference to the experience. Evidence of plan in relation to future practice.

TABLE 5-2

PROMPTS TO JUMP-START REFLECTIVE WRITING

_____ motivated me to. . .

I thought. . ., but. . .

I believed that. . .

_____ has made me question. . .

The question this raises for me is. . .

I always assumed that. . .

On the basis of. . ., I assumed. . .

_____ makes me feel like. . .

I feel/felt that. . .

I realized that. . .

_____ makes/made me realize that. . .

My expectation was that. . .

I wanted. . .

When it happened/didn't happen, I. . .

My views on. . . have been. . .

I imagined. . .

It surprised me to find out that . . .

_____ caused me wonder about. . .and that led me to. . .

_____ is important to me because. . .

_____ has affected the way I think/feel about. . .

What's Next?

> In this domain, I need to build up my resources and materials in order to provide my students with different avenues to learn. I understand that with time, I will be able to collect a library of resources to use with my students.

Those who are new to reflective writing often have trouble getting started. In order to help students jump-start their writing, we devised a set of writing prompts (Table 5-2). These can be used as practice exercises or as a "crib sheet" when working with Observation Follow-Ups or other tools.

A FINAL NOTE

Philosophy, the blueprint of the portfolio, and reflection, its defining feature, work hand-in-hand to clarify and express that which lies beneath the surface of your practice. The unseen forces — values and beliefs — that are exposed and examined through reflection find expression in your philosophy statement. Once known and shared, they can become powerful tools in strengthening your practice and making it more informed and intentional.

Chapter 6

Building a Portfolio

What we have to do is to be forever curiously testing new opinions and courting new impressions.

—Walter Pater

THE WHAT AND HOW OF SELECTING AND USING EVIDENCE

In this chapter, we explore and illustrate how criteria frame the portfolio structure and direct its content. We explain how criteria and portfolios are connected and show you the steps that will help you get from thinking and action to a finished document that represents both. As in previous chapters, we take the time to explain the meaning of well-worn, but often not well-defined terms in an effort to arrive at a common understanding for purposes of this text. *Evidence* is one such word.

WHAT IS EVIDENCE?

We use *evidence* as a broad-spectrum word to describe all of the components of the portfolio that support the builder's claims of competence with regard to knowledge, skills, dispositions, and accomplishments. We include in it every item that contributes to a reader's understanding of you as a professional. We divide evidence into two general categories: personal documents and artifacts. Personal documents are descriptive of who you are. Artifacts are descriptive of what you know and can do. Table 6-1 identifies a sample of personal documents and artifacts. This is not meant to be a comprehensive list, nor are the items listed in order of importance or value.

TABLE 6-1

EXAMPLES OF EVIDENCE

Personal Documents	Artifacts
Resumes	Work samples
Philosophy statements	Observations
Reflections	Lesson plans and units
Professional development certificates	Photographs
Awards	Assessment plans
Evaluations	Field work logs or journals
Letters of reference	Audio or video clips
Certificates of membership in professional associations	Newsletters
Transcripts	Case studies
Professional growth plans	Parent handbook

Evidence is all about communication. You use it to represent and communicate connections between your beliefs and actions, thinking and doing, and artifacts and criteria. Evidence is the tangible proof that your beliefs and principles are being consistently practiced. It includes reflection on your learning and growth in relation to your practice. And it documents the connections you have made between the artifacts you collect and the criteria that you are trying to meet. Figures 6-1, 6-2, 6-3, 6-4, 6-5, and 6-6 show a variety of evidence that Juli used in her portfolio to document her development of infant-toddler curriculum and the education and involvement strategies she employed with the children's parents. Figures 6.1 and 6.2 are examples of personal documents — Juli's reflections on her overall professional growth and on her more specific learning and development related to her work with infant and toddler curriculum. Figures 6.3–6.6 show examples of artifacts Juli included that validate her competency in several standards. The standards she met through the work represented in these artifacts and personal documents are shown in Figure 6-7. The next section of this chapter offers guidelines that will assist you in developing, collecting, and using evidence effectively.

GENERAL GUIDELINES FOR SELECTING AND USING EVIDENCE

We have identified five general guidelines for selecting and using evidence that apply to every type of portfolio. These include:

1. All evidence should express the voice of the builder.
2. All evidence should connect back to, and support, the purpose of the portfolio.
3. Each piece of evidence should be weighed against criteria to determine best fit.

4. Evidence must be explained to clearly communicate connections and relevance to criteria and/or philosophy.

5. The body of chosen evidence should be evaluated to ensure balanced coverage of all criteria.

Reflection on Professional Growth

Upon entering this cohort, my mindset was to complete the required classes and get my degree. I was not at all expecting to leave this cohort with not only such a dramatic change within my professional life, but also my home life. Every class that I have taken in this option has affected the center that I work in. From developing trainings to conducting a case study, I have been given the opportunity to affect the center in a positive way. This nontraditional class has had a far greater impact on me than any class that I have taken before. I have formed friendships with people who have given me insight to different ways of interpreting information when dealing with children, their families, and their community. Most importantly, they have now become a wonderful resource for me.

I use to be a child-care provider who thought her way was the only way, this narrow mindedness coming solely from my own like experiences. I am now a child-care provider who opens herself to the many possibilities, and even if I may not agree with certain differences, I still respect them.

Hernandez Family

Figure 6-1. Juli's Reflection on Personal Growth.

Reflection on my journey to find an appropriate curriculum for infants & toddlers

Before taking part in this program, I had never fully comprehended the concept of what a curriculum for an infant and toddler program should look like. With all the child development classes I had taken, only one or two focused on infant and toddler care. Curriculum wasn't even mentioned. When using curriculum with infants and toddlers, it was always similar to preschool curriculum. Now I know that infant/toddler curriculum is different than in a preschool setting.
Curriculum for infants and toddlers revolves around attachment and routines.
When putting this type of curriculum into practice, the child's individual needs for nurturing, security, and learning will be met.

Figure 6-2. Juli's Reflection on Infant and Toddler Curriculum.

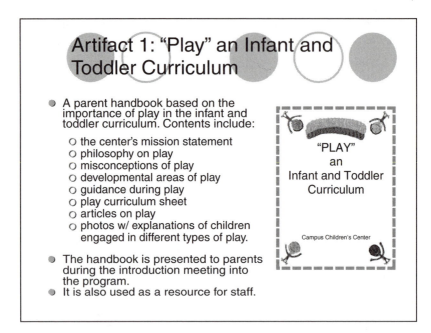

Figure 6-3.   Juli's Parent Handbook on Curriculum.

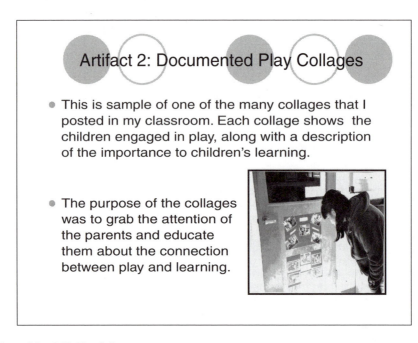

Figure 6-4.   Juli's Play Collages.

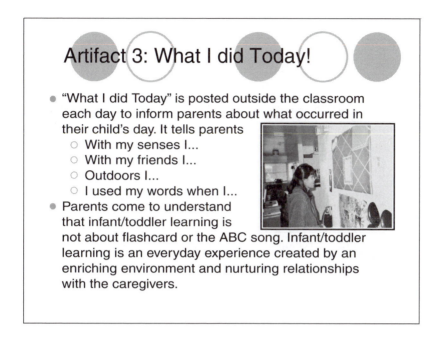

Figure 6-5. Juli's "What I Did Today!" Board.

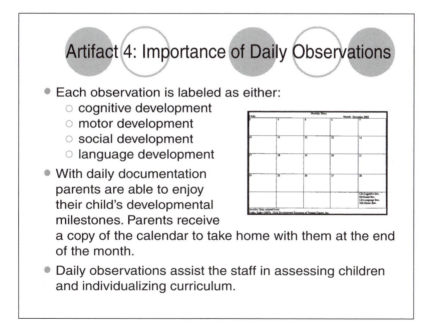

Figure 6-6. Juli's Daily Observation Log.

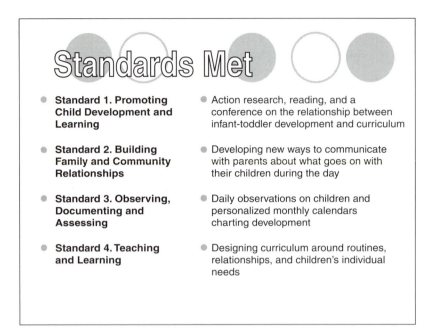

Standards Met

● **Standard 1. Promoting Child Development and Learning**	● Action research, reading, and a conference on the relationship between infant-toddler development and curriculum
● **Standard 2. Building Family and Community Relationships**	● Developing new ways to communicate with parents about what goes on with their children during the day
● **Standard 3. Observing, Documenting and Assessing**	● Daily observations on children and personalized monthly calendars charting development
● **Standard 4. Teaching and Learning**	● Designing curriculum around routines, relationships, and children's individual needs

Figure 6-7. Standards Met in Juli's Infant-Toddler Curriculum Project.

All Evidence Should Express the Voice of the Builder

The evidence is an honest and accurate representation of *your* work, learning, and accomplishments at a given point in time. Even though there may be others who interact with you in your learning process and learning environments — coteachers, instructors, master teachers, supervisors, and the like — the evidence is about you and your understandings and practices. The bottom line is that the portfolio — through the evidence — must reflect you and be congruent with your philosophy. At times we all find ourselves faced with the dilemma of being asked or expected to behave in ways that are inconsistent with our philosophies. This is not an uncommon occurrence. Although this can prove challenging, particularly in situations where you do not have ultimate control, you must remain true to yourself. The brief example below illustrates such a situation relayed by Kendra, who was engaged in building a portfolio for a college course. She had recently been hired at a child-care center to coteach a group of three-year-olds with a teacher who had been practicing for years.

> *Helen, my coteacher, got an art experience ready for the children. The night before, she had made a sample of a collage for the children to follow. It had a brown tree trunk, a green top, and five red circles she said were apples. She insisted that the children place the precut apples on the top of precut trees just like the sample. Each child could only have five circles*

and one tree. The children were supposed to put the apples on small dabs of glue that the teacher put on the paper. The children couldn't even decide where the glue went. Even though I helped the children with the project, it bothered me that it was so structured and controlled. It didn't even seem like any fun for anyone.

Helen's "one right way" approach conflicted with Kendra's philosophy of a more creative, child-directed approach. Successfully addressing this situation with Helen, and later addressing it in her portfolio, required tact, professionalism, and reflection-in-action. Kendra followed through with the art project as prescribed by her coteacher. In her portfolio, Kendra included two art samples: the one Helen had planned and a subsequent project she had planned. Without casting aspersions on Helen or her philosophy, Kendra compared the two projects in relation to her own philosophy, pointing out why hers was more congruent than the other with her beliefs about the way children learn. The reflection that accompanied the art samples in her portfolio demonstrated Kendra's mindfulness in a difficult situation, her insights, and her flexibility.

Later in the day, I asked Helen if she always does art this way. She said she does. She said it helps children learn to follow directions and learn about how things really look. She said this was a very important part of preschool. She seemed so sure about what she believes. I realized that I don't believe the same things she does about the purpose of art. I didn't want to tell her that her way is wrong, and I didn't want her to tell me that either. What she said made me think about what I do believe about art and what I think preschool is about.

After a while, we talked again. I explained that I like more open-ended art experiences because they allow children to be creative, make decisions about how they want their pictures to look, and explore the materials. I asked her if we could switch off doing art — she could plan it one week and I would plan it the next week. That way, the children could have different kinds of experiences that would teach them different things. She agreed, and I was so relieved. Now I feel like we can each do what we think is right and the children will benefit.

Through that experience, Kendra examined her beliefs and questioned her practice in light of the practice of her coteacher. Her reflection-in-action enabled her to introduce a compromise while still respectfully accepting Helen's point of view. She used the art samples to draw comparisons between different educational philosophies, making clear why she favored hers. So, while her artifacts included an art project that did not fit her philosophy, she used supporting evidence — her explanation and reflection — to clarify the inconsistency and to show her thinking, reasoning, decision making, connection making, and planning. It showed who *she* is in the context of her immediate circumstances.

TABLE 6-2

PORTFOLIO TYPES AND PURPOSES, AND THE NATURE OF THEIR
RESPECTIVE EVIDENCE

Type	Purpose of Portfolio	Nature of the Evidence	Samples of Evidence
Developmental	Facilitate and chart development	Selected sample showing incremental learning and growth over time in specific areas	Multiple drafts of philosophy statement, serial observations, reflective writings
Showcase	Highlight performance and capabilities	Projects that illustrate integration of knowledge, skills, and dispositions articulated across criteria	Parent handbook; staff training plan on play in the preschool curriculum
Assessment	Provide a basis for evaluation of competence in relation to teaching standards	Best work in all content areas specified in standards	Photographs of bulletin board showing completed K-W-L chart with caption explaining K-W-L procedure and how it connects to standards, lesson plans, class newsletter, assessment plans
Professional	Provide a basis for evaluation in relation to job or promotion requirements	Selected sample showing qualifications in relation to job requirements	Philosophy statement accompanied by evidence that demonstrates implementation of the philosophy; letter to parents, professional development certificates

All Evidence Should Connect Back to, and Support, the Purpose of the Portfolio

Keep the purpose of the portfolio in mind as you select representative evidence. Just as you will gauge evidence against your philosophy statement to determine coherence and consistency between them, you must also evaluate the relevance of evidence in terms of how well it helps you meet the purpose of the portfolio. Cognizance of your audience and the expectations they have can help you stay focused on the purpose. Table 6-2 summarizes portfolio types and purposes, and the nature of their respective evidence.

Each Piece of Evidence Should Be Weighed Against Criteria to Determine Best Fit

Portfolios are not about quantity. Each piece of evidence you select must do its part in telling your story — clearly demonstrating who you are, what you know, and what you can do in relation to the criteria you must meet. Matching evidence with criteria can be a painstaking process. It often requires you to sort through piles, boxes, and folders of saved items, all the while reflecting on what you are trying to say and show. It is a mindful, reflective process that has a strong impact on the quality of the finished product and the meaning you make of it. Criteria for a given portfolio may range from an open-ended guideline suggesting possible items for inclusion to a very prescriptive and comprehensive list of specific skills, knowledge and/or dispositions that you are required to demonstrate. No matter which criteria are in use, each piece of evidence must be very clearly connected to them.

Evidence Must Be Explained to Clearly Communicate Connections and Relevance to Criteria and/or Philosophy

Your reason for including each entry should be made transparent to the reader. Your purpose is to draw clear connections between the evidence and the specified criteria that form the backbone of the document. Whether in print or electronic format, each piece of evidence must be explained. The explanations serve to describe the context in which evidence was derived. It also lets the reader know how the evidence connects to a particular standard. The sample portfolio page (Figure 6-8) shows how explanations and artifacts work together to inform the reader.

NAEYC Sub-Standard 4d. Building meaningful curriculum
Use own knowledge, and other resources to design, implement, and evaluate meaningful, challenging curriculum that promotes comprehensive developmental and learning outcomes for all young children.

Explanation
My infant/toddler curriculum focuses on exploration of the environment, relationships between caregivers and the children and routines. These pictures focus on design and implementation of infant/toddler curriculum.

Cohl is exploring three bears. He is learning about texture and shape through his senses. He is also using his body to reach and balance and grasp the objects. He is practicing eye-hand coordination. (Sitting out of camera range) I encourage him, cheer him on, and name what he is doing ("Oh, Cohl, you are really reaching for those bears. Look what you have — a blue bear"). This promotes language development.

Reflection
I realize more and more that curriculum with infants is about helping them become more competent and secure and providing them with interesting, safe activities that challenge them. They keep me thinking about what else I can do to promote their development.

Figure 6-8. Explanations and Artifacts Working Together.

The Body of Chosen Evidence Should Be Evaluated to Ensure Balanced Coverage of All Criteria

Although specifications for breadth and depth of coverage of criteria may vary, your task is to ensure that all criteria to which you are held are adequately addressed. Often portfolio builders have strengths in some areas and are more challenged in others. It is reasonable to expect that areas of strength might tend to be overrepresented, inadvertently leaving more difficult or less favored areas wanting. Keep your strengths, challenges, and preferences in mind as you develop, collect, and compile evidence. Remember that every part of the criteria has its rightful place in the portfolio and needs to be addressed thoroughly in a convincing and meaningful manner.

Two strategies may prove useful to you in ensuring and examining coverage of the criteria: (a) create a filing system that allows you to sort and store evidence by criterion. This can help you avoid the problem of having an abundance in favored areas and little to none in less favored ones; (b) use a Portfolio Preparation Worksheet to inventory your evidence. We have provided a sample worksheet (Figure 6-9) that we use with students who are working with the California state standards. This tool is easily adapted to any criteria. It can be expanded to include subcategories or elements within each standard to accommodate more detailed inventorying.

California Standards for the Teaching Profession	Evidence I already have	Element/Standard that evidence supports	Evidence still needed
1. Engaging and Supporting			
2. Effective Environments			
3. Subject Matter			
4. Planning Instruction			
5. Assessing			
6. Professional Development			

Figure 6-9.   Portfolio Preparation Worksheet.

CHARACTERISTICS OF PORTFOLIO TYPES THAT INFLUENCE YOUR CHOICES OF EVIDENCE

As described in Chapter 3, each type of portfolio has characteristics that make it distinct from the other types. These characteristics have ramifications for your choices of evidence. We will address each type of portfolio in turn and discuss implications for evidence in relation to the unique characteristics of each.

Developmental Portfolios

Developmental portfolios are most often seen in the context of classroom settings as course assignments or as part of participation grades. Adult developmental portfolios are most akin to the portfolios teachers use in classrooms to document children's growth and development. These portfolios are used as formative assessment tools that provide guidance to the teacher and adult learner with regard to learning needs. Adult developmental portfolios contain selected samples of evidence showing incremental learning and growth over a specified period of time. Developmental portfolios include, as a mainstay, works in progress and multiple drafts of the same assignment, as well as finished products. They are used by the instructor, in conjunction with the adult student, to assess progress and plan for continuing improvement. Of course, all of these are supported and tied together by reflections. In the case of developmental portfolios, the philosophy statement may be an element, but often as a work in progress.

Developmental portfolios are most often constructed using criteria that are idiosyncratic to a particular instructor or mentor. In some cases, criteria are negotiated or coconstructed with the portfolio builder. The tasks represented in developmental portfolios are designed to build or refine basic competencies in such things as observation, reflection, research, and planning. This prerequisite competency building is done concurrently with activities geared to expand and deepen content knowledge. The prerequisite knowledge, skills, and dispositions practiced and honed in the developmental portfolio are later employed by the portfolio builder to accomplish tasks and projects in order to demonstrate mastery of external criteria as required in showcase, professional, and assessment portfolios.

Examples from a Developmental Portfolio

The curriculum of the child development option for early care and education practitioners at our university is aligned with the National Association for the Education of Young Children (NAEYC) Standards for Programs (2003). The standards are shown in Figure 6-10. Each course in the curriculum addresses one or more of the NAEYC standards. Developmental portfolios are used in some courses as a means for students to develop specific knowledge, skills, and dispositions that they will use in course projects and will later employ in the projects and products that will form their showcase portfolios.

The following example illustrates how Densie demonstrated, in her developmental portfolio, incremental progress in her ability to conduct detailed, descriptive, nonjudgmental observations of children. This skill was later applied in a case study in which detailed, serial observations of a particular child were used to demonstrate competency in NAEYC Standard 3 — Observing, Documenting, and Assessing to Support Young Children and Families.

Standard 1. Promoting Child Development and Learning
Candidates use their understanding of young children's characteristics and needs, and of multiple interacting influences on children's development and learning, to create environments that are healthy, respectful, supportive, and challenging for all children.

Standard 2. Building Family and Community Relationships
Candidates know about, understand, and value the importance and complex characteristics of children's families and communities. They use this understanding to create respectful, reciprocal relationships that support and empower families, and to involve all families in their children's development and learning.

Standard 3. Observing, Documenting, and Assessing to Support Young Children and Families
Candidates know about and understand the goals, benefits, and uses of assessment. They know about and use systematic observations, documentation, and other effective assessment strategies in a responsible way, in partnership with families and other professionals, to positively influence children's development and learning.

Standard 4. Teaching and Learning
Candidates integrate their understanding of and relationships with children and families; their understanding of developmentally effective approaches to teaching and learning; and their knowledge of academic disciplines to design, implement, and evaluate experiences that promote positive development and learning for all children.

Sub-Standard 4a. Connecting with Children and Families
Candidates know, understand, and use positive relationships and supportive interactions as the foundation for their work with young children.

Sub-Standard 4b.Using Developmentally Effective Approaches
Candidates know, understand, and use a wide array of affective approaches, strategies, and tools to positively influence young children's development and learning.

Sub-Standard 4c. Understanding Content Knowledge in Early Education
Candidates understand the importance of each content area in young children's learning. They know the essential concepts, inquiry tools, and structure of content areas including academic subjects and can identify resources to deepen their understanding.

Sub-Standard 4d. Building Meaningful Curriculum
Candidates use their own knowledge and other resources to design, implement, and evaluate meaningful, challenging curriculum that promotes comprehensive developmental and learning outcomes for all young children.

Standard 5. Growing as a Professional
Candidates identify and conduct themselves as members of the early childhood profession. They know and use ethical guidelines and other professional standards related to early childhood practice. They are continuous, collaborative learners who demonstrate knowledgeable, reflective, and critical perspectives on their work, making informed decisions that integrate knowledge from a variety of sources. They are informed advocates for sound educational practices and policies.

Figure 6-10.   NAEYC Initial Licensure (Core) Standards.

Denise

The guidelines for Denise's developmental portfolio required that she conduct at least 5 hours of observation of preschool children at play over the course of 5 weeks. In preparation for this, she and her fellow students were instructed in how to write running records. They explored the differences among description, interpretation, and judgment, and engaged in guided practice using video clips and follow-up discussion. In class each week, the students reviewed each other's observations using a rubric. With the instructor, the group explored, questioned, and clarified their work with a focus on how they could improve their observation technique. Figure 6-11 shows excerpts from Denise's observations and feedback she received from her peers and instructor. This example illustrates the progression of Denise's work on observations.

In the reflection following her fifth observation, she wrote,

Observation #1	Feedback
Sarah looks for another toy. She gets bored so she doesn't stay with any activity or toy very long before moving to something that appears to be more interesting. Sarah picks up a stacking toy that Joshua definitely wants and he takes it from her. Sarah becomes upset and starts to cry. The teacher makes him give the toy back and tells him he must share....	Remember to describe the actions of the children without interpreting their motives or feelings. Describe the behavior and/or body language/facial expressions that gave you the impression that she was bored or that the toy appeared more interesting, but don't assume how she feels. What behavior made you think Joshua definitely wanted the toy? Maybe it wasn't about the toy. Maybe he wanted Sarah's attention. Can you know this, or is it a guess? Stick to what you see, not to what you think happened.
Observation #5	**Feedback**
Angie and Marcie were in the dramatic play area. Angie said to Marcie, "You sit here. You be the one to eat and I will make lunch." She handed Marcie a child-produced book about food and said, "What do you want for lunch?" Marcie opened the book and pointed to a picture of spaghetti. She said, "Do you have this?" Angie answered, "Yes we do." She turned quickly and skipped to the sink. She took out a plastic carrot and cauliflower. She put them on a plate and walked slowly back to the table, carefully balancing the vegetables. She put the plate on the table in front of Marcie. Marcie looked down at the plate and frowned. Then she looked up at Angie with a half-smile on her face. She said in a loud voice, "That's NOT spaghetti." Angie answered, "It's the only spaghetti we have." Marcie replied, "I don't like that kind. I want pizza." Angie said firmly, "You can't have something else until you eat this." Marcie pushed away from the table, stood up, and with her hands on her hips, said, "I'm going to another restaurant."	Good use of descriptive words. You conveyed the feelings or intentions. I could really see the play unfold. You captured the children's dialogue very well. You let their words and expressions tell the story.

Figure 6-11. Excerpts of Observations and Feedback.

This is definitely getting easier. I don't feel like I have to write down every single thing in order to capture what is happening. I'm really keeping in mind description, description, description! I've gotten much better about not assuming what the children are thinking or intending. I'm focusing on really seeing what they're doing. Now, I'm paying much closer attention to my feelings about what I see vs. what I see and knowing the difference. I can't imagine teaching now without observing.

At the end of the 5-week period, Denise compiled her observation work samples and reflections for her developmental portfolio. When taken as a whole, the evidence showed clear proof of growth in her observation skills. Her reflections documented the evolution of her thinking about observation as it relates to her and as it relates to teaching. In her final reflection on the observation experiences, she made connections between where she had come from (in terms of using this skill), what she could do now, and how this skill would contribute to her practice in the future.

I thought I really understood observation before I started this process. Now I see how much I missed before and how much I assumed about what was happening without realizing it. This is much harder than it looks. Now when I observe the children, I keep asking myself, "What am I really seeing — and what do I think I'm seeing?" Now I know the difference and I know the questions to ask myself. I think being a better observer will make me a better teacher because this is really helping me not label the children. Now, I'm trying harder to understand them and how what's going on around them affects them. I've realized that sometimes play problems I think the children have are really the result of the dysfunction of the classroom or lack of staff being in tune with the needs of the children. I know now that I must make time in my everyday practice to observe the children and document what I see. This experience has shown me how useful observation is as a teaching tool.

Developmental Portfolios as Preparation for Showcase or Assessment Portfolios

As we pointed out above, developmental portfolios often constitute preparatory work. They focus on acquisition and refinement of knowledge, skills, and dispositions that students will later employ as they set about the work of demonstrating competencies. Figure 6-12 provides an example of the relationships between a developmental portfolio, a showcase portfolio, and criteria. The column labeled "Developmental Portfolio" summarizes a set of competency-building tasks (shown in bold) that students practiced as part of their developmental portfolios: observation, analysis, and reflection. These skills, once mastered, were available to students as they designed and implemented their showcase portfolio projects. Column 2 — Showcase Portfolio — shows the outline that Denise used to plan and execute her case study of Marissa. Each of the skills that she refined through the developmental portfolio was employed and resulted in evidence, in her comprehensive project in the showcase portfolio: observation, analysis, and reflection (also shown in bold). The third column — NAEYC Standards — identifies the specific standards addressed in the portfolio entry in which the skills observation, analysis, and reflection are embedded.

Showcase Portfolios

Showcase portfolios, like their developmental cousins, are somewhat idiosyncratic. Their criteria are often formulated at the program level rather than being designed by an instructor. These portfolios often constitute part of a graduation requirement internal to the institution conferring the degree or certificate. Although external standards, such as those promulgated by professional associations, frequently provide the framework for this type of portfolio, these entities have no evaluative function with respect to the institution in this regard. For instance, the degree option for practitioners, mentioned above, uses NAEYC's Standards for Programs (2003) as the criteria for students'

Developmental Portfolio: Competency-Building Tasks	Showcase Portfolio: Denise's Portfolio Entry Outline	NAEYC Standards
Observe preschoolers using specimen & running record methods. Conduct a series of five 30-minute field observations on play behaviors in young children. Record your observations with attention to completeness, objectivity, specificity, mood, and directness (Curtis & Carter, 2000). **Analyze** play behaviors using specified theoretical perspectives. **Reflect** on each observation experience noting where you started in your skill & understanding of observation, what you learned about yourself and your practice through the observation experience, how you will use your learning in future practice.	**Case study of Marissa:** • Assessing play problems & supporting play entry and prosocial play skills • Standards this project addresses & how it does so. • Major learning achieved through execution of the project Evidence that demonstrates competencies: **Personal documents** Reflections, narrative re: connection to philosophy **Artifacts** Observations, assessment of child's play behaviors, summaries of planning & follow-up meetings with coteachers, report from parent conference, video clips of Marissa playing with peers, intervention strategies to support play entry and prosocial play skills, assessment of strategy outcomes and report of future plans. How each artifact illustrates learning & demonstrates competency	**Standard 3. Observing, Documenting, and Assessing to Support Young Children and Families** Know about and understand the goals, benefits, and uses of assessment. Know about and use systematic observations, documentation, and other affective assessment strategies in a responsible way, in partnership with families and other professionals, to positively influence children's development and learning. **Standard 4. Teaching and Learning** Candidates integrate their understanding of and relationships with children and families; their understanding of developmentally affective approaches to teaching and learning; and their knowledge of academic disciplines to design, implement, and evaluate experiences that promote positive development and learning for all children. **Sub-Standard 4a. Connecting with children and families** Candidates know, understand, and use positive relationships and supportive interactions as the foundation for their work with young children.

Figure 6-12. Relationships Between a Developmental Portfolio, a Showcase Portfolio, and Criteria.

showcase portfolios. Whereas teacher credential candidates' assessment portfolios (addressed later in this section) require coverage of each element within each state standard, showcase portfolios, as we use them, are comprised of up to six comprehensive projects. Each of these projects integrates and reflects multiple, broadly defined national standards. Showcase portfolio builders exercise a high degree of autonomy in determining portfolio content. As these students are all working professionals in early care and education, their projects correspond directly to the needs and demands of their work environments and professional interests and development.

Figures 6-13–6-18 depict a project from Kathryn's showcase portfolio. She developed a comprehensive curriculum project that she implemented with her preschool group and their families — all residents of a small, rural town in the heart of farm country in California's Central Valley. Kathryn's curriculum project had four dimensions: (a) the development of integrated, topically and culturally relevant curriculum for four-year-olds in her classroom; (b) staff development for the staff in her center; (c) parent education on developmentally appropriate curriculum and play in the classroom; and (d) parent involvement. The standards her project addressed are shown in Figure 6-13

Standards Addressed in Kathryn's Curriculum Project

Standard 2. Building Family and Community Relationships
Candidates know about, understand, and value the importance and complex characteristics of children's families and communities. They use this understanding to create respectful, reciprocal relationships that support and empower families, and to involve all families in their children's development and learning.

Standard 4. Teaching and Learning
Candidates integrate their understanding of and relationships with children and families; their understanding of developmentally effective approaches to teaching and learning; and their knowledge of academic disciplines to design, implement, and evaluate experiences that promote positive development and learning for all children.

Sub-Standard 4b. Using Developmentally Effective Approaches
Candidates know, understand, and use a wide array of effective approaches, strategies, and tools to positively influence young children's development and learning.

Sub-Standard 4d. Building Meaningful Curriculum
Candidates use their own knowledge and other resources to design, implement, and evaluate meaningful, challenging curriculum that promotes comprehensive developmental and learning outcomes for all young children.

Standard 5. Growing as a Professional
Candidates identify and conduct themselves as members of the early childhood profession. They know and use ethical guidelines and other professional standards related to early childhood practice. They are continuous, collaborative learners who demonstrate knowledgeable, reflective, and critical perspectives on their work, making informed decisions that integrate knowledge from a variety of sources. They are informed advocates for sound educational practices and policies.

Figure 6-13.   Standards addressed in Kathryn's curriculum project.

Integrated Curriculum Unit

I used two different webs to plan the farm curriculum. The first web is for content areas (literacy, music & movement, math, science, art, and social studies). The second web focuses on the children's developmental needs (intellectual, physical, social, and emotional). By using both of the webs I can make sure I have considered the whole child and can easily tell if the curriculum plan is well balanced and integrated.

Farm Curriculum

Click here to view Farm Unit Curriculum ▶

Figure 6-14.   Kathryn's Integrated Farm Unit.

Kathryn addressed Standard 2 by selecting as the basis for her curriculum unit the farm-life experiences of the children and families with whom she works. By doing so, she validated their experience as a valuable subject worthy of

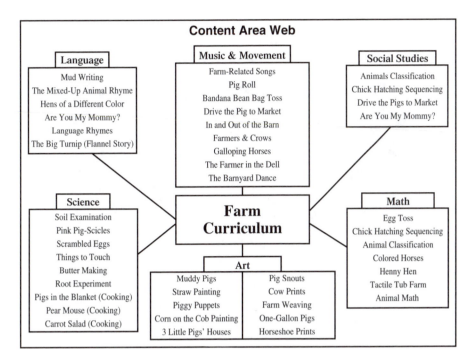

Figure 6-15. Kathryn's Content Area Web.

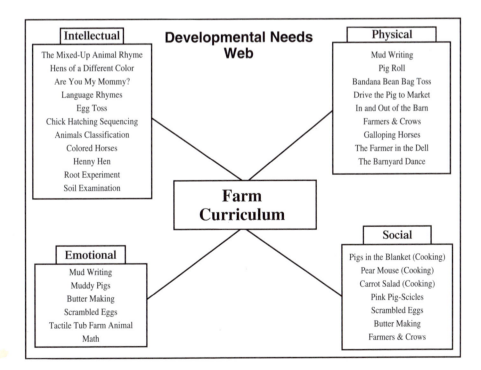

Figure 6-16. Kathryn's Developmental Needs Web.

Figure 6-17. Kathryn's Parent Night Presentation.

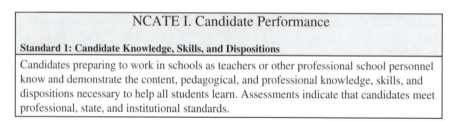

Figure 6-18. NCATE I. Candidate Performance.

investigation in the classroom. She invited the parents to participate in a variety of ways throughout the implementation of the unit. Kathryn demonstrated competence in Standard 4, particularly 4b and 4d, through her inclusion of numerous teaching strategies, activities, and tools that spanned and connected developmental domains and content areas. Kathryn planned, implemented, and evaluated two activities that focused on Standard 5: an in-service training for the center staff on integrated curriculum, and a presentation for parents. Both of these activities explained and promoted developmentally appropriate curriculum and play in the classroom. Notice the small icons on the bottom right corners of Figures 6-14 and 6-17. Kathryn prepared her portfolio in electronic format using PowerPoint presentation software. The icons link to additional sources of evidence that explain and support her project. Electronic portfolios will be discussed in Chapter 7.

We showed, in the section above, how developmental portfolios are used to build foundational knowledge, skills, and dispositions that can later be used in showcase portfolios. Developmental portfolios are not limited, however, to this use. They can be employed as proficiency-building devices in any learning context.

The showcase portfolio is an affective communication tool, particularly when the display of multifaceted projects is the goal. Now, we turn to portfolios used for evaluation purposes. You will recall from Chapter 3 that there are two types of portfolios used for evaluation: assessment and professional.

Assessment Portfolios

Assessment portfolios are most commonly used in academic settings, particularly those that involve teacher credentialing and other types of specialized preparation. They are also used to obtain national teacher certification. Criteria that govern assessment portfolios vary by source (e.g., national professional associations, state licensing agencies). Criteria can be very broad or highly specific. In any case, assessment portfolios are intended to show competence in all areas specified in the criteria to which they are subject.

We have included a brief discussion of criteria related to teacher credentialing and other specialized preparation in order to draw the differences between them as they affect portfolios. Being knowledgeable about the criteria, or levels of criteria, to which you will be held accountable is a crucial step in portfolio success. That knowledge will guide you in your selection of evidence and prepare you for its eventual assessment. As a starting point, we have provided an overview in Table 6-3 of the standards and the categories of professional preparation to which they connect.

TABLE 6-3

CATEGORIES OF PROFESSIONAL PREPARATION AND SETS OF STANDARDS

	NCATE	NAEYC Core Standards	NAEYC Advanced Standards	State Teaching Credential Standards
Initial teacher credentialing with accreditation in early childhood education (K–3)	yes	yes	no	yes
Advanced preparation (specialist, Master's in early childhood education)	yes	yes	yes	no

Having a sense of the relationships among various sets of standards can be helpful when trying to translate criteria into action plans that are then reflected in your portfolio. Keep in mind that the standards to which you will be held are determined by your institution and the political landscape of your state or region.

Now to the standards. National accrediting bodies, such as the National Council for Accreditation of Teacher Education (NCATE) and the NAEYC have come to be seen in education as the standard-bearers of quality. These bodies accredit teacher preparation and advanced programs in higher education. The standards set by such bodies directly influence the content of assessment portfolios in accredited programs. Not all of these programs are accredited, nor do all accredited programs require portfolios.

The NCATE standard shown in Figure 6-18 is an example of criteria that pertain specifically and directly to teacher candidate and advanced preparation. It relates directly to candidate performance criteria and provides guidance as to portfolio content.

In addition to being an accrediting body in its own right, the NAEYC is a specialty professional association (SPA) recognized by NCATE as the body that defines the standards for early childhood education. Teacher preparation programs with a K–3 emphasis that are NCATE/NAEYC accredited adhere to both NCATE standards and NAEYC core standards for initial licensure of teachers. The NAEYC core standards were previously shown in Figure 6-10.

Accredited institutions that grant advanced certificates and degrees in early childhood education adhere to NCATE standards, and both the core and advanced standards set by NAEYC. "[A]t the advanced level, candidates demonstrate competence at a higher level and with greater depth and specialization" (Hyson, 2003, p. 76). These candidates do not address state teaching credential standards but are "expected to hold an initial license in early childhood education or a closely related field" (Hyson, 2003, p. 76). The NAEYC advanced standards are shown in Figure 6-19.

In addition to these national accreditation standards, teacher-preparation programs are subject to requirements specified by their individual state agencies responsible for teacher credentialing. This does not necessarily apply to advanced preparation programs. Although NCATE and NAEYC standards are well aligned with each other, state standards are not always as well aligned with those at the national level. The California Standards for the Teaching Profession, Figure 6-20, are a case in point. The national standards contain elements specific to the education of young children, ethics, and advocacy, whereas the California state standards do not.

At the institutional level, teacher-preparation programs, in conjunction with their respective states, define how they will meet their state requirements for assessment of teacher candidates. The institution may determine that it will use portfolios as one method to assess student learning. This is the case at our university. Some programs within the teacher-education

---

NAEYC ADVANCED STANDARDS

I. CORE STANDARDS (shown on Table 10 above)

II. ESSENTIAL PROFESSIONAL TOOLS FOR ALL CANDIDATES IN ADVANCED PROGRAMS.

1. Cultural Competence: Advanced program candidates demonstrate a high level of competence in understanding and responding to diversity of culture, language, and ethnicity.

2. Knowledge and Application of Ethical Principles: Advanced program candidates demonstrate in-depth knowledge and thoughtful application of NAEYC's Code of Ethical Conduct and other guidelines relevant to their professional role.

3. Communication Skills: Advanced program candidates possess a high level of oral, written, and technological communication skills, with specialization for the specific professional roles (s) emphasized in the program.

4. Mastery of Relevant Theory and Research: Advanced program candidates demonstrate in-depth, critical knowledge of the theory and research relevant to the professional role (s) and focus area (s) emphasized in the program.

5. Skills in Identifying and Using Professional Resources: Advanced program candidates demonstrate a high level of skill in identifying and using the human, material, and technological resources needed to perform their professional roles and to keep abreast of the field's changing knowledge base.

6. Inquiry Skills and Knowledge of Research Methods: Using systematic and professionally accepted approaches, advanced program candidates demonstrate inquiry skills, showing their ability to investigate questions relevant to their practice and professional goals.

7. Skills in Collaborating, Teaching, and Mentoring: Advanced program candidates demonstrate the flexible, varied skills needed to work collaboratively and effectively with other adults in professional roles.

8. Advocacy Skills: Advanced program candidates demonstrate competence in articulation and advocating for sound professional practices and public policies for the positive development and learning of all young children.

9. Leadership Skills: Advanced program candidates reflect on and use their abilities and opportunities to think strategically, build consensus, create change, and influence better outcomes for children, families, and the profession.

III. ADDITIONAL SPECIALIZED COMPETENCIES:

Beyond the core standards and essential professional tools, programs may identify additional competencies essential to particular focus areas or specializations. Examples might be knowledge of the legislative process for candidates specializing in public policy and advocacy, or skills in personnel and fiscal management for candidates in an early childhood administration program. Programs with such additional competencies should identify them in clear performance language and include criteria by which the program assesses these competencies.

(Hyson, 2003, p. 77)

Figure 6-19. NAEYC Advanced Standards.

program use portfolios to assess student learning and readiness for the teaching profession.

In the sections that follow, we provide examples from portfolios fitting the two categories of standards: those that tend to be broad (national standards) and those that are very specific, such as the state standards found in California. Knowing the standards that govern your portfolio will enable you to use these examples to your best advantage.

Assessment Portfolios for Initial Teaching Credential

The students in our early childhood credential program prepare a portfolio that is organized around the state's six standards for the teaching profession (Figure 6-20). The process of building an assessment portfolio based on these standards prepares students to do what is expected of them as new teachers in

CALIFORNIA STANDARDS FOR THE TEACHING PROFESSION

STANDARD ONE: ENGAGING & SUPPORTING ALL STUDENTS IN LEARNING	STANDARD TWO: CREATING & MAINTAINING EFFECTIVE ENVIRONMENTS FOR STUDENT LEARNING
1.1 Connecting students' prior knowledge, life experience, and interests with learning goals 1.2 Using a variety of instructional strategies and resources to respond to students' diverse needs 1.3 Facilitating learning experiences that promote autonomy, interaction, and choice 1.4 Engaging students in problem solving, critical thinking, and other activities that make subject matter meaningful 1.5 Promoting self-directed, reflective learning for all students	2.1 Creating a physical environment that engages all students 2.2 Establishing a climate that promotes fairness and respect 2.3 Promoting social development and group responsibility 2.4 Establishing and maintaining standards for students 2.5 Planning and implementing classroom procedures and routines that support student learning 2.6 Using instructional time effectively
STANDARD THREE: UNDERSTANDING & ORGANIZING SUBJECT MATTER FOR STUDENT LEARNING	**STANDARD FOUR: PLANNING INSTRUCTION & DESIGNING LEARNING EXPERIENCES FOR ALL STUDENTS**
3.1 Demonstrating knowledge of subject matter content and student development. 3.2 Organizing curriculum to support student understanding of subject matter 3.3 Interrelating ideas and information within and across subject matter areas 3.4 Developing student understanding through instructional strategies that are appropriate to the subject matter 3.5 Using materials, resources, and technologies to make subject matter accessible to students	4.1 Drawing on and valuing students' backgrounds, interests, and developmental learning needs 4.2 Establishing and articulating goals for student learning 4.3 Developing and sequencing instructional activities and materials for student learning 4.4 Designing short-term and long-term plans to foster student learning 4.5 Modifying instructional plans to adjust for student needs
STANDARD FIVE: ASSESSING STUDENT LEARNING	**STANDARD SIX: DEVELOPING AS A PROFESSIONAL EDUCATOR**
5.1 Establishing and communicating learning goals for all students 5.2 Collecting and using multiple sources of information to assess student learning 5.3 Involving and guiding all students in assessing their own learning 5.4 Using the results of assessments to guide instruction 5.5 Communicating with students, families, and other audiences about student progress	6.1 Reflecting on teaching practice and planning professional development 6.2 Establishing professional goals and pursuing opportunities to grow professionally 6.3 Working with communities to improve professional practice 6.4 Working with families to improve professional practice 6.5 Working with colleagues to improve professional practice 6.6 Balancing professional responsibility and maintaining motivation

Figure 6-20. California Standards for the Teaching Profession.

the California public schools. The content for these initial portfolios is highly prescriptive; students must document competence for all of the standards and elements of the standards. We have included a variety of samples from portfolios that illustrate how students have documented their competence in initial licensure standards.

Laurel's Portfolio

Laurel used artifacts from her student teaching experience to document her competence in Standard 1.1 — Connecting student's prior knowledge, life experiences, and interests with learning goals. To document competence in this element, Laurel used a copy of a third-grade student's written work in which he described his prior experiences with teeth as part of a unit on dental health (Figure 6-21). The writing activity helped the student connect his prior knowledge and real-life experiences with teeth to his new learning in the health unit. The content of the health unit also provided a focus for working on writing skills.

The Tooth Traditions artifact documents the connection between a specific element of the standard and the classroom activity that Laurel designed and implemented with the children to demonstrate her competency. Laurel used a series of artifacts to document her work in relation to the various elements of this standard. After assembling the artifacts, Laurel wrote the following reflection. The reflection — a personal document — is part of the evidence that illustrates her growth as a professional as it relates to this standard.

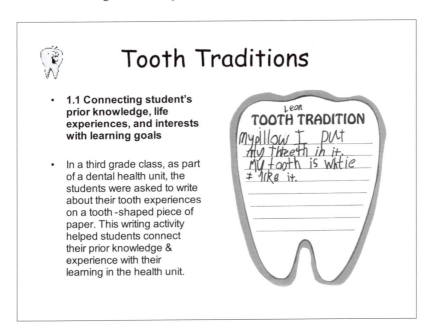

Figure 6-21. Tooth Traditions.

Laurel's Reflection

Engaging and Supporting All Students in Learning
Where I started

> I started out believing that this was an easy standard to achieve, that engage-
> ment was just students paying attention and that supporting was monitoring. I
> thought this standard would be met if students were looking at me and I was
> looking back.

Where I am now

> I now know that much more is needed in order for this standard to be met.
> Engagement is active involvement in meaningful activities or curriculum. In
> order to engage and support all students in the learning process one must
> connect to their prior knowledge, use a variety of strategies in order to meet the
> needs of all students, and provide activities that make subject matter meaning-
> ful. Having the students' attention is not enough.

Where I'm going

> I feel that I have come a long way in this area, but realize there is still more to
> learn. I plan to develop in this area by attending in-service sessions, staff devel-
> opment workshops, and through the help of my BTSA support provider and
> school staff.

Laurel's reflection conveys her personal gains from having done the set
of activities related to Standard 1, of which Tooth Traditions was a part. At
the same time, the act of writing reflections demonstrates competence in
Standard 6.1 — Reflecting on teaching practice and planning professional
development.

Elsewhere in her portfolio, Laurel used personal documents as sources of
evidence to show competence in Standard 6.2 — Establishing professional
goals and pursing opportunities to grow professionally. One example was a
certificate of participation for helping to plan, organize, and present a session
at a local conference (Figure 6-22).

Assessment Portfolios for Advanced Candidates

Assessment portfolios for advanced candidates meet NCATE standards and
NAEYC Core and Advanced Standards. Students meeting these standards generally have more autonomy with regard to portfolio development than do teacher
credentialing candidates in that they are guided by national standards, which
are more open-ended and less prescriptive than some states' requirements.
The examples we have included from portfolios of candidates in advanced
programs serve to demonstrate how broad standards can be addressed.

Standard Six:
Developing as a Professional Educator

6.2 Establishing professional goals and pursing opportunities to grow professionally.

Certificate of participation for helping to plan, organize, and present the session: "Ethical Dilemmas! What's that got to do with teaching?"

Figure 6-22. Personal Document: Certificate of Participation.

The table of contents shown in Figure 6-23 is from the portfolio of Lori, a preschool teacher and master's student. She developed the portfolio as part of her supervised fieldwork placement the semester before doing her final master's project or thesis. Lori's table of contents reflects her flexible, creative approach to the broad national standards. Note the item "My Philosophy in Action." This is an item of Lori's own invention.

Lori used "My Philosophy in Action" to clearly illustrate how her philosophy guides her teaching. Her artifacts, which include scanned images of children's written work and parents' notations on the work, corroborate her philosophy (Interactive Journal: home–school collaboration, Figure 6-24). With regard to these journals, she wrote, "Parents scaffold the children's developing writing by translating their beginning writing into standard writing for the teacher. Children read their entries to the teacher upon returning to school."

Through this evidence, Lori provided documentation for a variety of standards:

> NAEYC Standard 2 — Building family and community relations
> NAEYC Standard 4 — Teaching and learning
> NAEYC Essential Professional Tool 7 — Skills in collaborating, teaching, and mentoring

By meeting these NAEYC standards, Lori simultaneously provided documentation for her work in NCATE's Standard 1. The Interactive Journals became a medium through which Lori involved parents in the school life of their children. It validated the parents as the children's first

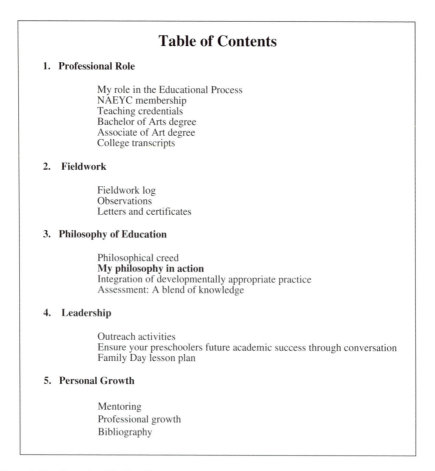

Table of Contents

1. **Professional Role**

    My role in the Educational Process
    NAEYC membership
    Teaching credentials
    Bachelor of Arts degree
    Associate of Art degree
    College transcripts

2. **Fieldwork**

    Fieldwork log
    Observations
    Letters and certificates

3. **Philosophy of Education**

    Philosophical creed
    My philosophy in action
    Integration of developmentally appropriate practice
    Assessment: A blend of knowledge

4. **Leadership**

    Outreach activities
    Ensure your preschoolers future academic success through conversation
    Family Day lesson plan

5. **Personal Growth**

    Mentoring
    Professional growth
    Bibliography

Figure 6-23.   Example of Table of Contents.

teachers. It created a meaningful collaboration between the parents and teacher, promoted ongoing dialogue between home and school, and allowed children to see that their parents value education. At the same time, the activity helped the children develop literacy skills and creative expression. It also provided an opportunity for children to work with their parents on a meaningful task.

Sometimes artifacts are construed as only those things that relate to, or depict, children's activities. The Interactive Journal example used above is that kind of artifact. Artifacts are also those items that the portfolio builder uses to conduct the business of their own learning, however, such as field experience logs. Figure 6-25 is an excerpt from a field-experience log that another master's student, Brenda, included in her portfolio.

In addition to artifacts, personal documents constitute evidence of fulfillment of criteria. Brenda's Personal Growth Plan provides such evidence. Figure 6.27 shows the introduction to the plan that Brenda included in her electronic portfolio. Within the introduction, Brenda embedded links that take

Sample of Interactive Journals:
A home–school collaboration

- Parents scaffold the children's developing writing by translating their beginning writing into standard writing for the teacher. Children read their entries to the teacher upon returning to school.

Figure 6-24. Interactive Journal: Home–School Collaboration.

Date	Hours	Site	Age/Grade	Participation/Observation
2/17/04	12:00 – 3:00 pm (3hrs)	Sunset	5–8 year-olds K–3	Participation in "Girls Grow Strong" in Girl Scouting! Learning about "Healthy Moves" and expressing feelings. Songs and games. (NAEYC Exceptional Professional Tools 7) (EPT 7)
2/12/04	12:00 – 3:00 pm (3hrs)	Sunset	5–8 year-olds K–3	Showing respect for others means treating them the way you want to be treated. Meeting people. Different eating customs, songs, and games, and the Promise and Law. (NAEYC EPT 1,2)
2/18/04	12:00 – 3:00 pm (3hrs)	Del Mar	5–8 year-olds K–3	Participation in activity: singing, stretch arms and legs by touching the ground. Observed monitoring staff interaction with the children. (NAEYC Standard 5)
2/24/04	12:00 – 3:00 pm (3hrs)	Sunset	5–8 year-olds K–3	Model hygiene routines for girls — washing hands and combing hair. Songs and games — Tarzana and Great Big Moose (NAEYC Standard 1)

Figure 6-25. Brenda's Field Experience Log.

the reader to the actual Personal Growth Plan. Chapter 7 will cover electronic portfolios.

Brenda's Personal Growth Plan documents progress toward meeting NAEYC Standard 5 — Growing as a Professional. In developing her plan, she had to consider steps she would need to take to continue her professional growth. This began with a self-assessment of her beliefs in light of exemplary practices in early childhood education. She then identified an area of special interest to pursue. Her final step in developing the plan was to identify her

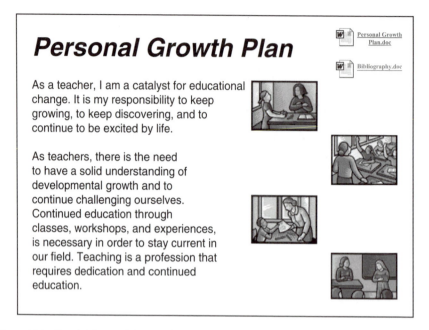

Figure 6-26. Brenda's Personal Growth Plan Introduction.

short- and long-term goals, create a timeline, and select readings applicable to her area of interest.

As you can see from the section above, assessment portfolios accommodate a wide variety of standards with varying degrees of prescriptiveness. They are the most common type used for evaluation, but not the only type. Professional portfolios are also used for evaluative purposes. We will discuss two types of professional portfolios in the next section: those that are used for job seeking and those that are used when seeking promotion.

Professional Portfolios

Professional portfolios are primarily used in employment contexts: when applying for a position or seeking promotion. The content of professional portfolios reflects the requirements set out by employers, just as developmental, showcase, or assessment portfolios reflect requirements set out by their guiding authorities: an instructor, an institution, a state credentialing body, or a professional association. Unlike other types, however, professional portfolios often contain items not particularly specified by employers, but which are nonetheless informative.

Portfolios Used for Job Seeking

The professional portfolio is one of several tools employers might use to determine the best fit for a given position. Sometimes they are used as a prescreening device. They can also be used as a visual aid in an interview session. It can be assumed that employers in educational settings, as a rule, would expect a portfolio to contain, at a minimum, a resume, a philosophy statement, and letters of reference. Beyond these items, employers vary in their expectations. Job descriptions often provide excellent guidance as to what to include in the portfolio. Employers' Web sites or print materials are also good sources of information for portfolio planning. They may give you insights into employment culture/policies/programs to which you might decide to address a portion of your portfolio content.

In building a professional portfolio for interview purposes, put yourself in the place of the employer. Consider what you would want to know about an applicant that would help you make a good hiring decision. At the same time, consider the length of the document. Your goal is to present your background convincingly yet concisely. We recommend including the following sections and items:

1. Cover page
2. Table of contents
3. Professional Background:

This section of the portfolio includes personal documents that describe who you are professionally. Take care in considering how much to include. The quality and substance of the documentation, from the standpoint of the reader, is important to keep in mind. We think the essentials include:

- your philosophy statement
- current resume
- permits, licenses, certificates, and/or clearances
- letters of recommendation
- unofficial, but complete, transcripts
- professional growth plan
- awards and certificates related to professional development and service
- anything else specified by the employer (first aid or CPR certification)

You may wish to include additional items in an appendix, such as other permits or licenses that you think strengthen the case you are making about your ability to do the job, acknowledgments of participation in professional associations and conferences, and letters of appreciation for profession-related service.

4. Professional Practice:

This section of the portfolio should include carefully selected artifacts that demonstrate your knowledge, skills, and dispositions appropriate to the type of employment you are seeking. Figure 6-27 provides a sample job description with examples in the adjacent column of artifacts you might use to demonstrate one's competence.

Sample Lead Preschool Teacher Job Description	Location and Examples of Evidence in the Portfolio
Responsibilities	
The care, safety, and well-being of all children in the group	Professional Background: Resume. Detail your previous experience in which you were responsible for groups of children
Planning and implementing developmentally appropriate curriculum for preschoolers	Professional Background: Philosophy statement. Professional Practice: A web of an integrated curriculum unit, an outline of a curriculum project, a summary of curriculum activities in a content area such as literacy, a lesson plan
Setting up the physical environment to meet the changing needs and interests of the children and in accordance with health and safety requirements	Professional Background: Philosophy statement. Professional Practice: Photographs, with narratives, of environments you have managed and shaped
Modeling best practice and ethical practice as defined by NAEYC	Professional Background: Philosophy statement. Professional Practice: Best practice can be addressed in the brief narratives that accompany curriculum, staff development, and parent involvement artifacts
Participating in regular staff meetings and other professional development activities	Professional Background: Certificates of conference participation, awards, etc. Professional Practice: Summary of contributions you have made toward staff development in previous positions
Maintaining positive relationships and regular communication with parents	Professional Background: Philosophy statement. Professional Practice: Parent newsletter
Supervising assistants, parent volunteers, and other classroom personnel as required	Professional Background: Resume noting supervision responsibilities Professional Practice: Photographs, with narratives, of parent involvement in the classroom
Working as part of a team	Professional Background: Philosophy statement. Professional Practice: Flyer and photographs, with narratives, of center festival, fundraiser, parent night, staff training, letter of appreciation
Professional Background	
AA in child development or equivalent	Resume
Courses/certification required to meet state requirements	Certificates, transcripts
2 years of full-time experience as a teacher or assistant teacher in early care and education	Resume and letters of recommendation
Current certification in child CPR	Certificate
General knowledge of nutrition and first aid	Resume
Good health as verified by a physician's statement	Health form or letter from physician on letterhead
Tuberculosis clearance	Certificate
Fingerprint clearance	Photocopy of fingerprint card or other acceptable form

Figure 6-27.   Sample Job Description with Examples of Artifacts.

The four types of portfolios we have discussed — developmental, show-case, assessment, and professional — can be adapted to suit almost any need builders might have with regard to documenting their professional growth and development. Regardless of purpose or type, however, a portfolio will most likely be subject to one or more reviews. In the section that follows, we dis-cuss the kinds of reviews that are common to portfolios.

Portfolios Used for Promotion

Portfolios have become widely accepted as tools to assess students' develop-ment and learning at all levels — from infancy through graduate school. The value of this practice has not been lost on administrators where employee development and competency are concerned. Increasingly, assessment by port-folio is being adopted as a means to determine an employee's promotability in the employment setting. Guidelines for promotion portfolios vary widely. In some instances, employers are highly prescriptive — indicating in great detail, the numbers, kinds, and levels of activities to be included. On the other end of the spectrum, promotion guidelines can be quite general — asking the candidate to represent the experiences that they believe characterize their readiness for a new level of responsibility as they perceive it. Regardless of criteria, promo-tion portfolios can provide an excellent vehicle for reflection and goal setting.

In preparing a promotion portfolio, you might consider including the following topic areas:

> Philosophy of education
> Pedagogical approach
> Global reflection on professional growth
> Curriculum vitae (all relevant experience and education)
> Accomplishments
> Evidence (personal documents and artifacts)

ASSESSMENT: FORMATIVE AND SUMMATIVE LOOKS AT PORTFOLIOS

Each of the portfolio types we have described is designed to present an accu-rate point-in-time portrait of its builder. Each has its unique characteristics, and yet each holds characteristics in common. One of the things it holds in common is that all portfolios undergo some form of review or assessment. For purposes of this discussion, we first want to clarify a few terms associated with assessment.

The words *assessment* and *evaluation* are often used interchangeably in the literature to mean measuring or assigning comparative value in relation to cri-teria or in a ranking. Sometimes these words are differentiated. *Assessment* is used when describing progress toward a goal but without assigning value; evaluation is used to mean assigning value, as in the first definition.

We use the word *assessment* throughout this book, and we distinguish between two types: formative and summative. We define *formative assessment* as descriptive of an ongoing process of review and revision toward a goal of mastery. For instance, a student may submit a draft of his philosophy statement. The student and instructor may use a rubric to determine the clarity and completeness of the statement, and identify areas for clarification or revision. Kilbane and Milman (2003) illustrate formative assessment with this characterization:

> imagine a chef tasting a soup while she is cooking it. Because the soup is still in its formative stage, the chef can change the recipe as needed to improve the soup. If the chef's goal is to produce a tasty soup, then all evaluation evolves around investigating this characteristic — not texture or color of the soup. (p. 80)

We define *summative assessment* as assigning value and making a determination of quality against external criteria. It describes where a person is in relation to a specific set of skills, a knowledge base, or dispositions at a given time. It is a measure of whether, or the degree to which, a person has achieved proficiency. Outcomes, such as the awarding of a grade for an assignment or course, result from summative assessments. Kilbane and Milman (2003) illustrate summative assessment in this way:

> imagine a crowd at a dinner party tasting and deciding how well they like the soup the chef has made. At this point, it is too late for the chef to improve the soup. It is left up to the crowd to judge its quality. They each have ideas about what quality means. Each will decide how well the soup measures up to their idea of what soup would taste like, look like, and smell like. Then sometimes the crowd will make a judgment about how good the chef is based on her soup. (p. 80)

Portfolio builders, who are familiar with the assessment tools that will be applied to their portfolios, are in a position to make informed decisions regarding content and presentation. The type of assessment employed will depend on the purpose for which the portfolio was designed, or where it is in the process of being developed. For instance, a rubric might be used for formative assessment as the portfolio is being developed. Revisions will be aimed at bringing the quality of the portfolio to a higher level on the rubric. The same rubric might then be used for summative assessment. Grades or other decisions will be based on the finished product. In the following section we discuss rubrics, checklists, and peer and instructor critiques. We have included examples of each of these tools.

RUBRICS

Rubrics are frequently used as tools to assess a piece of work's level of quality. Rubrics present a continuum of scoring criteria with descriptions that identify the levels of quality. One advantage of using rubrics is that those who will be judged by them have the final assessment criteria to use as a guide while developing their portfolios. Another advantage of rubrics is that they provide the assessor with a tool that helps ensure a greater measure of consistency and standardization across multiple portfolios. Table 6-4 shows a scoring rubric for portfolios that we adapted from Montgomery and Wiley (2004). We have organized ours using three levels: developing, competent, and accomplished. *Developing* indicates minimum, yet adequate proficiency. *Competent* reflects a level of accomplishment beyond the basics, indicating substantial grasp of content. *Accomplished* illustrates the highest level of synthesis and integration, effective communication, thoroughness, and a firm grasp of the complexities of teaching and learning

We have included a second rubric, shown in Figure 6-28, that is notable in two ways: (a) the criteria it measures are shown on the same page as the rubric, and (b) it has four levels of quality rather than three, as shown in the Portfolio Scoring Rubric. We use it with final student teachers in an early childhood credential program. The students are given the rubric at the beginning of the semester and are encouraged to use it as a guide while developing their course portfolio. It is later used by the supervisor in a summative assessment of the portfolio.

CHECKLISTS

Checklists provide guides for keeping track of the completion of required components and/or steps in the procedure. They are often used for self-pacing and sequencing of tasks; they are also used by mentors and instructors to monitor students' progress. This type of tool provides an organized way to keep track of what has been done and what remains to be done. The checklist in Figure 6-29 can be helpful as you plan and develop your portfolio.

Most of the items on the checklist are covered in other parts of this book. We have included a special note about timelines, however. Keep in mind that portfolio development often ends up requiring much more time than you might anticipate. Include in your timeline the applicable items from the checklist. Be sure to plan in time to review the final document and make revisions or modifications as needed. If a due date is associated with the portfolio, you might find it helpful to begin with that date and work backward.

TABLE 6-4

PORTFOLIO SCORING RUBRIC

Content	Developing	Competent	Accomplished
Evidence (artifacts and personal documents)	Few artifacts and personal documents are related to one or more of the standards, and connections between evidence and criteria may be murky. Evidence of professional practice is sometimes unclear.	Most artifacts and personal documents are related to one or more of the standards, and connections are logical and clear. Evidence of professional practice is provided.	All artifacts and personal documents are clearly and directly related to one or more of the standards, and very clear connections are made between all evidence and criteria. Strong evidence of professional practice is provided.
Captions	Captions sometimes do not clearly convey the intent of the writer.	Captions are clear on careful reading. Some captions are difficult to understand.	Captions clearly communicate meanings without contradiction.
Reflections	A few reflections indicate insights and make connections to impact of learning and meaning to future actions.	Most reflections show insight and connections to past and present learning and experience with meaning to future actions.	Highly insightful. Thoughtful connections among past and present learning/experience. Delineates implications for future action. Shows evidence of projection and planning.
Organization	Organization is somewhat obscure. Navigation is challenging for the reader. Signage is inconsistent or in some cases not present. Content groupings are somewhat confusing.	Organization is unclear in places, requiring careful attention in order to navigate successfully. Signage is not always consistent or obvious. Content groupings are not always logical.	Organization facilitates ease of navigation and access to supplementary evidence. Signage (e.g., TOC, links, tabs) is clear and accurate. Content groupings are logically arranged.
Design and Layout	Graphic elements are not always complementary, sometimes confusing or distracting from the message.	Graphic elements are mostly complementary, adding interest and enhancing the message.	Graphic elements are used judiciously; they enhance the message and add a dynamic quality to the finished product.
Writing mechanics	Use of standard English, yet frequent errors in spelling, grammar, and syntax make reading difficult.	Use of standard English, but writing has some errors in spelling, grammar, and syntax.	Excellent use of standard English with no errors in spelling, grammar, or syntax. Writing is fluid, clear, and coherent.

Source: Adapted from Montgomery, Wiley, *Creating E-Portfolios Using PowerPoint*, 2004.

EHD 160, Option II, final student teachers

Course Assessment Portfolios:
(Later adapted for Interview and *BTSA)

Content Criteria

Reflection for each of the six domains/standards of the California Standards for the Teaching Profession.
Reflection can be written using the Past, Present, Future model.
At least 1 example of supporting evidence for each element for each standard.
Clear connections from evidence to elements.

Organization and Presentation Criteria

Six sections, one for each domain of the California Standards.
Title/cover page, table of contents, tabs, neat, organized, typed, grammar/spelling.

	Content	**Organization and Presentation**
Inadequate	Meets less than half the requirements.	Looks careless and/or hurried, parts illegible. Multiple grammatical and stylistic or spelling errors.
Satisfactory	Each domain has a reflection and at least one piece of supporting evidence for each element.	Content is typed but presentation appears rushed. Some errors in grammar and/or spelling but they do not interfere with clarity.
Strong	Insightful reflections for each domain, all artifacts clearly connected to elements.	Clear, uncluttered, and attractive. Easy to find specific information. Few grammatical and/or stylistic or spelling errors.
Outstanding	All domain reflections show growth and learning from experience, feedback, and readings.	Evidence that pride and care were taken, and the message of product is clearly defined. Nearly error-free, reflecting clear understanding and thorough proofreading. Very user friendly.

*BTSA: Beginning Teacher Support and Assessment Program

Figure 6-28. Rubric for Final Student Teachers in Early Childhood Credential Program.

Checklist for Portfolio Development

Check when the item shave been completed

Stage 1. Preparation

____ Determine purpose, type, context, and audience
____ Develop timeline
____ Decide on print or electronic format, or both
____ Develop a budget
____ Collect artifacts and personal documents that already exist
____ Develop artifacts and collect additional personal documents as needed
____ Select exemplars from body of evidence to include in portfolio

Stage 2. Building the portfolio

____ Title page
____ Table of contents (Categories for organizing content)
____ Self-introduction
____ Philosophy statement
____ Global reflection on professional growth
____ Project description (if applicable)
____ Reflections on subsections (as is appropriate)
     (individual standards or project)
____ Evidence (artifacts and personal documents) — with explanation and connection to criteria

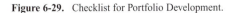

Figure 6-29. Checklist for Portfolio Development.

PEER AND INSTRUCTOR FEEDBACK CRITIQUES

It is the practice in many programs to provide opportunities for peer feed-back on portfolios, in addition to that of instructors. These critiques can be used to provide assessment on parts of portfolios — partitive critiques — during the development phase of the work. They can also be used to assess the whole portfolio. In either case, the assessments can be either formative or summative.

When used to assess parts of portfolios, such as a teaching unit or a project, critiques are more narrowly focused on how the evidence meets a particular goal or standard/s within the criteria. When used to assess the whole portfolio, the focus is on how well the completed work conveys the message of competence in relation to the full criteria. Although peer or instructor critiquing may not be part of your setting, you can use this tool as a means of self-assessment. We have included a partitive critiquing form in Figure 6-30.

Portfolio Entry Critique			
Presenter		Critique by	
Portfolio entry		Date	
Standard/s addressed			
Criteria	**Rate 1 – 5 (1 = high)**	**Strengths and Suggestions for Improvement**	
The intended audience/user of the activity or project is clear	1 2 3 4 5		
The purpose of the presentation or product is clear	1 2 3 4 5		
The evidence demonstrates strong connections to the identified standard/s	1 2 3 4 5		
The evidence clearly demonstrates competence (accomplishes the purpose)	1 2 3 4 5		
If supplementary evidence is used (e.g., items for inclusion in an appendix), it is consistent with the standard/s	1 2 3 4 5		
The content is well organized (follows logically with good connections throughout)	1 2 3 4 5		
The content is attractively and professionally presented	1 2 3 4 5		

Figure 6-30. Portfolio Entry Critique.

A FINAL NOTE

Constructing a portfolio involves many challenges and opportunities. The ultimate challenge is to present unequivocal documentation that you know and can do what is specified in the criteria to which you are subject. This is no easy task. It requires diligence, perseverance, and focus. The challenges can seem formidable. And yet, there is much to be learned from taking them on. The opportunities lie in rising to the challenge. Portfolios offer the possibility of deep, personally meaningful learning that only comes about through a solid investment of time, energy, will, and commitment. Satisfaction lies in a job well done.

Chapter 7

Structure, Design, and Construction of Print and Electronic Portfolios

Creative work is play. It is free speculation using materials of one's chosen form.

—Stephen Nachmanovitch

How many times have you picked up a book or magazine only to put it back down because it just did not appeal to you? Maybe the pages were too busy or the print was too crowded and small. Like books and magazines, portfolios are publications. The more appealing they are, the better chance they have of being read and taken seriously. This chapter is dedicated to helping you make choices necessary to creating a professional, finished product, whether in electronic or print form. We have included some general guidelines that apply to both formats, followed by guidelines and suggestions specific to each format. But first you must decide which format you will use for your portfolio: print or electronic.

PRINT OR ELECTRONIC FORMAT?

Portfolios can be created in print or electronic format. In some cases, an instructor or program criteria will determine the format for you. In cases where you have a choice, you will need to consider a number of factors before deciding which format better suits your needs. Each format has its pluses and minuses, as you will see below.

Print Portfolios

Print portfolios are composed of materials that will be quite familiar to anyone who has been to school. They are most often housed in three-ring binders, although file boxes and accordion files are also used. Section dividers, tabs, good-quality paper, and page protectors are also typically used in print port-folios. These materials are inexpensive and readily available.

The processes by which information is readied for inclusion in the portfolio will also be familiar. Artifacts and personal documents can be easily dupli-cated using a photocopier. We recommend that these items be duplicated in color where applicable, in order to preserve their original appearance. This would apply to items such as permits, certificates, and work samples. A cautionary note: Include copies of originals in your portfolio, rather than originals. Beyond the photocopier and word processor, support equipment is not necessary to create or view a print portfolio — no electricity or batteries required! Print portfolios are low-tech, requiring minimal technical skill on the part of the builder.

Print portfolios are stand-alone documents — what you see is what you get. This can be a plus or a minus. When the reader opens the portfolio, everything is there to see. No technical skill or know-how is required to move about and manipulate the pages. Because every item of support docu-mentation is physically present, however, the portfolio can be bulky and unwieldy, making navigation and continuity challenging. Reading the port-folio often requires the reader to flip back and forth to view evidence associ-ated with a particular topic. This physical manipulation can impair the sense of continuity and flow and become a distraction in and of itself. Other disad-vantages with print portfolios include storage and duplication. Print portfo-lios are bulky to store. They are also costly, in both time and materials, to reproduce for distribution.

Electronic Portfolios

Electronic portfolios (e-portfolios) present opportunities and challenges to builders and readers alike. On the opportunity side, e-portfolios are compact, easy to store and distribute, and inexpensive to duplicate. The hyperlink fea-ture common to e-portfolios makes navigating through them quite easy and efficient. It also facilitates a more flexible structure than is possible in print versions. Print versions necessarily follow a linear structure — one page fol-lows another. Support documentation is often in an appendix at the back, add-ing to the document's bulk, complicating navigation, and compromising continuity. Electronic versions allow the reader to move about the document at will. Their nonlinear structure means that support documentation can be virtu-ally attached where appropriate without compromising the overall continuity and flow of the document.

E-portfolios require access to technology, technical skill, and often a degree of technical support, which print versions do not. Readers must also have access to computer hardware and compatible software in order to read the portfolio. On the plus side, e-portfolios provide builders with an opportunity to display their technical competence — something that is now considered desirable or even essential in the contemporary teaching environment. Depending on the builder's knowledge of computers and familiarity with software applications, however, the learning curve can be quite steep, thus adding a measure of difficulty to the portfolio process.

Reproducing evidence for inclusion in an e-portfolio can be somewhat more complicated than doing it for print versions. Documents such as permits and work samples must be scanned, rather than photocopied, in order to create digital images that will then be accessible electronically. Some of these technical issues are discussed in greater depth later in this chapter.

Once the choice has been made to "go electronic," a further decision must be made as to which type of e-portfolio to create. E-portfolios fall into two main categories. The first is web based — those that are created for display over the World Wide Web. The second category is non-web based — those that are created using presentation software.

Web-Based Portfolios

Web-based portfolios are designed to be viewed via the Internet. The builder creates a web page on which to display the portfolio, and that web page is posted to a server. Software such as Microsoft Front Page is used to design web pages. Because web-based portfolios are stored on servers rather than on the user's own computer, there may be costs associated with renting storage space on a server.

Web-based portfolios present several unique challenges. The first involves level of technical skill. Although computers, in many cases, have become part of everyday life, web-page design is still well outside of the experience or expertise of many users. Time must be invested, above and beyond that needed to build the portfolio, in order to acquire web-authoring skills. Tools for creating web-based portfolios are becoming increasingly user-friendly, however. The second challenge has to do with accessibility. Web-based portfolios are potentially accessible by anyone anywhere in the world who has access to the Internet. Although Internet security is improving, it still must be considered, as portfolios often contain personal and contact information. Additionally, with web-based portfolios the intended readers of the portfolios must have Internet access, some degree of technical know-how in order to view them, and often passwords.

Non–Web-Based Portfolios

Non–web-based portfolios are created using presentation software. Once produced, they are saved to a CD-ROM or DVD. This makes them very portable, easy to distribute and store, and secure. The Internet is not a factor in this type of portfolio. The builder controls distribution by providing CDs or DVDs directly to the intended audience.

The simplest type of electronic portfolio is that used for developmental purposes. Developmental portfolios, as we use them, are often comprised of a set of electronic files and subfiles that are shared between the builder and the instructor or mentor. They are not configured on presentation software. All other portfolio types — showcase, assessment, and professional — require a more complex organizational structure. This structure is facilitated by presentation software.

PowerPoint is presentation software that is readily adapted to portfolio work. It is a software application within Microsoft Office, an integrated software package that includes, at a minimum, word processing (Word) and spreadsheet (Excel) applications. The integrated nature of this software facilitates easy transfer of documents created in one application (e.g., Word) to other applications in the same package (e.g., PowerPoint).

We prefer using PowerPoint with students, rather than web-based tools or other presentation software, for several reasons. First, most students have some familiarity with it and ready access to it. Second, because it is easy to learn and use, the amount of time a student spends to become reasonably proficient is minimal. This applies to those who are new to computers and also to those who have never used presentation software. Third, PowerPoint gives users a lot of flexibility and a range of tools for individualizing their documents. And fourth, because this software is so widely used, readers of portfolios are likely to have it available for viewing the documents.

STRUCTURING PORTFOLIOS

We have provided three outlines, shown in Table 7-1, to guide you in structuring your portfolio of choice: one for showcase portfolios, one for assessment portfolios, and one for professional portfolios used for job interviews. The outlines list the basic features that readers in various contexts might expect to find. You may decide to include others, and, of course, the criteria for your particular portfolio will act as a guide to your inclusions.

PORTFOLIO FEATURES FOR PRINT
OR ELECTRONIC PORTFOLIOS

Showcase, assessment, and professional portfolios hold some features in common, such as title pages/slides and statements of philosophy, whereas some features are unique to a particular portfolio type (shown in Table 7-1).

TABLE 7-1

OUTLINES FOR SHOWCASE, ASSESSMENT, AND PROFESSIONAL PORTFOLIOS

Showcase Portfolios	*Assessment Portfolios*	*Professional (Interview) Portfolios*
Title slide or page	Title slide or page	Title slide or page
Table of contents	Table of contents	Table of contents
Navigation map (used in electronic showcase or other portfolios in which clusters of standards are addressed in the same entry)	Self-introduction	Philosophy statement
Self-introduction	Philosophy statement	Resume
Philosophy statement	Global reflection	Permits, licenses, certificates, and clearances indicated in the job description
Global reflection on growth	Major learning achieved — slides or pages for each standard that relay learning associated with respective standard addressed	Letters of recommendation
Project description — a slide or page for each project that includes a brief description of the project and each standard addressed in the project	Evidence slides or pages — includes artifacts and personal documents, references to the standard/s or requirement/s, reflections associated with specific standards or projects	Transcripts
Major learning achieved — slides or pages for each project that relay learning associated with each standard the project addresses		Professional growth plan
Evidence slides or pages — includes artifacts and personal documents, references to the standard/s or requirement/s, reflections associated with specific standards or projects		Awards and certificates related to professional development and service
		Documentation of professional practice
		Any other documentation requested by the employer can usually be integrated into the above categories

The features we have included here are common to both print and electronic portfolios. Where the features of portfolio types are held in common, we have provided a single example below that can be applied to all. In the cases where features differ from one type to another, we have included samples for each portfolio type that address their uniqueness. You will notice that, in the examples, e-portfolio slides are shown in landscape, rather than portrait views. This is because PowerPoint uses landscape view exclusively in its lay-out of slides. The type and quantity of information you wish to display is better suited to some slide layouts than to others. Experiment with various layouts to determine which work best. We have used a variety of slide layouts in the e-portfolio examples that accompany the discussion of the features below. These examples will give you an idea of the possibilities available in PowerPoint.

Regardless of portfolio type, we remind you that the examples we have provided are just that — examples. Use them as a guide, but do not let them limit your imagination and creativity.

Title Page

Every portfolio type needs a title page/slide, just as every book needs a cover. The visual appeal of the title page/slide is important (Figure 7-1), because it provides an opportunity to make a good first impression. As with every page/slide in your portfolio, you can configure it to best show the information and deliver your message. Print portfolios are often contained in binders.

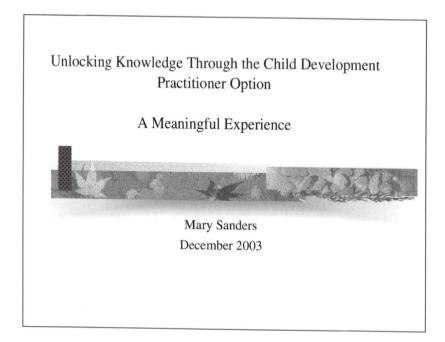

Figure 7-1. Title Slide.

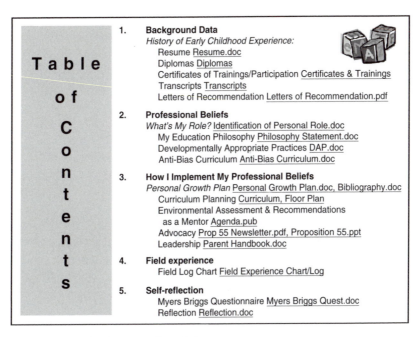

Figure 7-2. Linear Table of Contents, Example 1.

Presentation binders (those with transparent pockets on the outside front cover) work especially well, since the page inserted in the pocket can serve as both the portfolio cover and title page.

Table of Contents

Like the title page/slide, every portfolio type requires a table of contents. The table of contents will be different for each portfolio type, reflecting its unique features, organization, and entries. In each case, the table of contents has two main purposes. First, it informs the reader about what you have included in the document. Second, it tells the reader how you have organized the contents. Print portfolios use page numbers to indicate location of materials; e-portfolios use links in lieu of page numbers for navigation purposes. Links will be covered later in this chapter. We have included three variations on the e-portfolio table of contents. Figure 7-2 is from a professional portfolio. Figures 7-3 and 7-4 are both from showcase portfolios. Figures 7-2 and 7-3 are linear versions — that is, they are organized in an outline form, such as one you might find in a book. This format suggests movement through the document in a straight line. Figure 7-4 is in a nonlinear form. It is organized as a diagram or web, which invites moving about on the basis of interest.

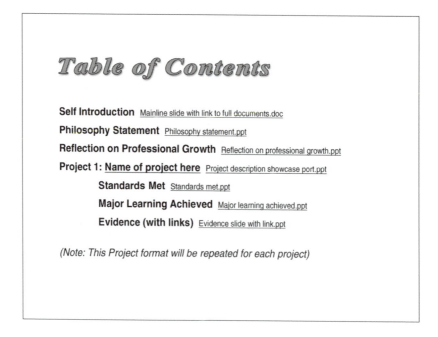

Figure 7-3. Linear Table of Contents, Example 2.

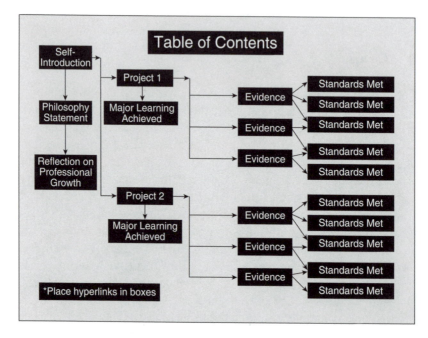

Figure 7-4. Nonlinear Table of Contents.

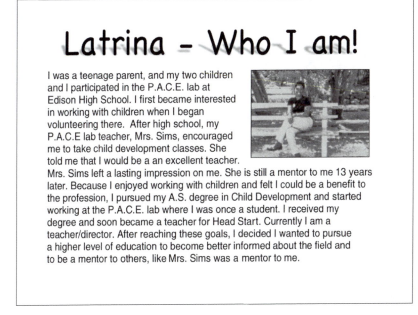

Latrina - Who I am!

I was a teenage parent, and my two children and I participated in the P.A.C.E. lab at Edison High School. I first became interested in working with children when I began volunteering there. After high school, my P.A.C.E lab teacher, Mrs. Sims, encouraged me to take child development classes. She told me that I would be a an excellent teacher. Mrs. Sims left a lasting impression on me. She is still a mentor to me 13 years later. Because I enjoyed working with children and felt I could be a benefit to the profession, I pursued my A.S. degree in Child Development and started working at the P.A.C.E. lab where I was once a student. I received my degree and soon became a teacher for Head Start. Currently I am a teacher/director. After reaching these goals, I decided I wanted to pursue a higher level of education to become better informed about the field and to be a mentor to others, like Mrs. Sims was a mentor to me.

Figure 7-5. Self-Introduction.

Self-Introduction

The self-introduction is another page/slide that every portfolio type includes. Shown in Figure 7-5, it offers readers a glimpse into who you are and gives them a chance to get to know you. Different portfolio builders approach the content of this in various ways. Some give it a personal slant; some give it a more professional slant. There is no "right way." You might provide a personal story about how and why you entered the early care and education field, or relay something of your professional goals. You might choose to talk about the intersection of your personal and professional lives. These and other approaches can be very effective. The approach you take should be guided by two things:

1. The purpose for which you are developing the portfolio — keep your audience in mind.

2. The type of content that you are most comfortable revealing — let your comfort level be your guide.

Philosophy Statement

Every portfolio type includes a philosophy statement. In an e-portfolio, space on a slide is limited. Therefore, depending on its length, you may choose to summarize it on this slide and include a link to the entire document. The slide layout shown in Figures 7-6 and 7-7 is useful for documents, such as a

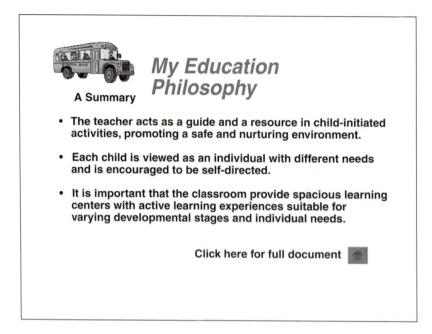

Figure 7-6. Philosophy Statement Summary with Link.

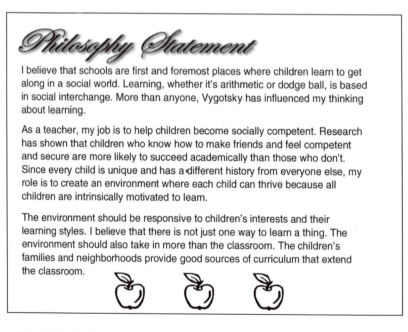

Figure 7-7. Philosophy Statement.

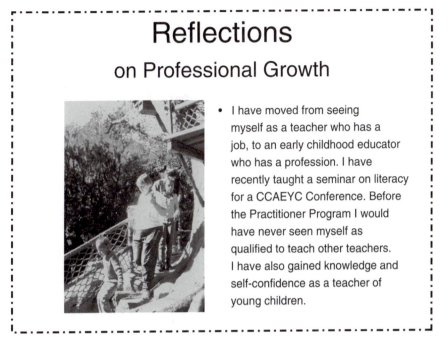

Reflections
on Professional Growth

- I have moved from seeing myself as a teacher who has a job, to an early childhood educator who has a profession. I have recently taught a seminar on literacy for a CCAEYC Conference. Before the Practitioner Program I would have never seen myself as qualified to teach other teachers. I have also gained knowledge and self-confidence as a teacher of young children.

Figure 7-8. Reflections on Overall Professional Growth.

philosophy statement, where text is the primary means of delivering information, as opposed to photographs or other graphics.

Reflection on Overall Professional Growth

Reflection is the defining characteristic of all portfolios. This type of reflection statement, as shown in Figure 7-8, is intended to provide an overview of your growth and change through your experiences as a student as part of a class or program (for showcase and assessment portfolios), or throughout your career thus far (professional portfolios). You will also provide reflections throughout the portfolio in conjunction with, and as part of, your evidence.

Project Description

Figure 7-9 conveys information about a specific project within a showcase portfolio. It contains a brief description of the project and identifies the standards that have been met through the project. Each project in the portfolio will have a project description.

Project 1: Assessing Desired Results

Project Description

This project focused on improving my management of the documentation process required for the California Department of Education Desired Results (DR). I felt that my observation process was fragmented and unintentional. Although the curriculum I provide develops the skills children need to meet DR, I did not effectively manage the documenting of those skills.

In this project, I set out to answer the question: How do I make lesson plans, the curriculum goals, and the daily assessment process manageable to accomplish systematic documentation of Desired Results?

Standards met in this project:
Standard 3 – Observing, documenting, and assessing…
Standard 4d – Building meaningful curriculum

Figure 7-9. Project Description.

Major Learning Achieved

Showcase and assessment portfolios contain slides addressing major learning achieved. In the case of a showcase portfolio, the content focuses on the learning achieved in relation to a particular project. In assessment portfolios, it focuses on the learning achieved through the conduct of various types of activities. In both cases, concentrate on the big ideas you came away with. You should present the details of your learning — what you know and can do — in the evidence section that follows (Figure 7-10).

Evidence

Evidence gives substance to your claims of competence. Every portfolio type includes evidence: personal documents and artifacts. Your captions and explanations tell the reader, for instance, what they are looking at, how you used it, with whom you used it, what you hoped to achieve through its use, and what it means in relation to the criterion it documents. It often takes more than one page/slide to present evidence. At the same time, however, it is important to be mindful of the total number of pages/slides you use. Keep this number

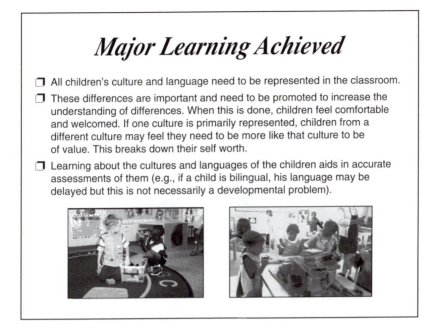

> ## *Major Learning Achieved*
>
> ❑ All children's culture and language need to be represented in the classroom.
>
> ❑ These differences are important and need to be promoted to increase the understanding of differences. When this is done, children feel comfortable and welcomed. If one culture is primarily represented, children from a different culture may feel they need to be more like that culture to be of value. This breaks down their self worth.
>
> ❑ Learning about the cultures and languages of the children aids in accurate assessments of them (e.g., if a child is bilingual, his language may be delayed but this is not necessarily a developmental problem).

Figure 7-10.   Culture and Language Emphasized

manageable for the reader. In e-portfolios, use hyperlinks on your mainline slides to connect the reader to additional documentation that can provide more complete evidentiary support when necessary. In print portfolios, use an appendix for additional document support documents.

Include graphics where appropriate. Let the reader see what you are talking about. A picture *can* be worth a thousand words if selected carefully. You might use photos of a group of children engaged in a project or lesson, photos of the workshop in which you delivered your presentation, children's work samples, or diagrams of your own design (Figure 7-11). Graphics make this part of the portfolio come alive.

RELEASE FOR PHOTOGRAPHS

Portfolio evidence frequently includes photographs of human subjects. As you prepare artifacts for inclusion in your portfolio, make sure that you have secured written permission from, or for, those whose images you capture in photographs, video, or film. If the subjects are children, written permission must be obtained from their parents or guardians. Figure 7-12 gives you an idea of what you might include in a form of your own design.

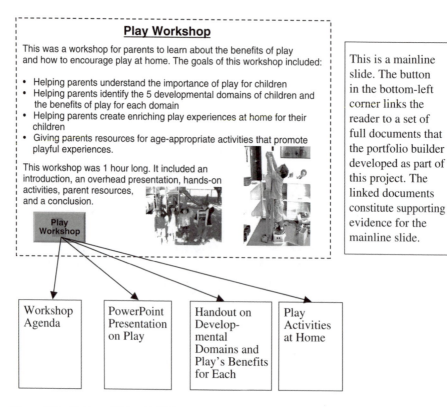

Figure 7-11. Evidence Slide with Link.

Photograph Release

I grant permission to_____to use my photograph and/or the photograph of my child, in publications developed and used for educational purposes. By signing this permission form, I am agreeing that there will be no compensation to me or my child for use of these materials.

I release_____ from liability that might stem from the inclusion of these materials in educational publications.

Name_____Child's name_____
  Print Name Clearly   Print Name Clearly

Signature_____

Address_____

Figure 7-12. Sample Photo Release.

DESIGN TIPS

We have included some tips to guide you in constructing your portfolio. Let your eye, and these tips, be your guide when designing your pages/slides.

Kilbane and Milman (2003) identify four principles of graphic design: contrast, repetition, alignment, and proximity. We have included a fifth principle: use of graphic elements. These principles work together to create a sense of balance, congruence, and professionalism in the finished product. They can also work against each other, creating products that confuse the eye or distract the reader.

Contrast refers to the degree of difference between graphic elements. Graphic elements consist of any item used on a page/slide (e.g., background color of the page or slide, text, pictures, colors, the sizes of objects, or the sizes or styles of fonts). An example of contrast is black print on white paper. The sharp contrast makes reading the text very easy. One of the most common errors is that made in e-portfolios when the background color of the slide and the color of the text are too similar (e.g., tan background with yellow text).

Repetition is another important principle. Repeating elements throughout your document helps create a sense of continuity and order. A consistent color scheme, background, and font and/or graphics that are similar in design help to unify the portfolio and keep it from looking like a patchwork of disconnected pages.

Alignment is the third principle to consider. This principle addresses the placement of elements on your pages/slides. The eye looks for symmetry or balance. Even asymmetrical configurations can convey a sense of balance. Alignment requires consideration of the whole space — edge to edge. Margins, blank space, and graphic elements must work together. In e-portfolios, pay special attention to margins and text/graphics box edges. PowerPoint does not recognize the edges of a slide in the way that a word-processing program recognizes the margins of a page. In PowerPoint, the boxes in which you position text and graphics will run off the edges of the slide, sending your text into parts unknown, if you overfill them or insert unnecessary page returns.

Proximity relates to how close graphic elements are to one another. Elements that are related to one another go together. Elements that are dissimilar should enjoy a separation. As Kilbane and Millman (2003) point out, "This grouping contributes to the organization of information for both the eye and the mind" (p. 139).

Use of graphic elements is of concern when designing a portfolio. Portfolio builders sometimes have a tendency to include too many graphic elements. While these can dress up a document and add interest, too much embellishment to background, font styles, word art, borders, stickers, or other elements can overwhelm your message. Use them with care.

SPECIAL DESIGN TIPS FOR POWERPOINT USERS

These tips are included to ease the transition to PowerPoint for those who may be unfamiliar with it. They include a brief explanation of how Power-Point treats font, the use of automation and sound effects, and the use of auto-play.

Font and font size defaults (automatic settings) on PowerPoint are set so that the text can be read from across a room. The default font is Arial; the default font size depends on the type of text box used. Title boxes default to 40-point font, subtitle boxes default to 32-point font, and text boxes default to 28-point font. In general, these size fonts are too large for use on portfolio slides. A font size of 16–18 points works well for body text in many fonts. Keep readability in mind when making your selections. Choose two or three fonts at the most, and use them consistently throughout your portfolio. The same goes for font sizes. Limit them to two or three. These limitations will help you avoid visual clutter.

Animation and sound effects available on PowerPoint are great fun. You can usually spot a document created by a new user because everything that jumps and sputters is included. Have fun experimenting with them, but use these features in your final document sparingly on individual pages and throughout the document. They should enhance your message and add interest, rather than detract from what you are trying to get across.

When using auto-play, allow enough time on each slide for the reader to read the content. Check this by having someone who is unfamiliar with it read it through for you, rather than timing it yourself. Your intimate knowledge of the content will enable you to read it faster than someone who is seeing it for the first time.

USING POWERPOINT TO CREATE AN ELECTRONIC PORTFOLIO

The idea of e-portfolios is new to many adults with whom we work. Some find the prospect exciting and challenging. Others approach it with trepidation or even fear. We have found that a few notes of explanation, some organizational guidance, and some design pointers are usually enough to get builders moving in the right direction. We have included all of these in the next sections.

Notes of Explanation

This is not meant to be a complete guide to using PowerPoint. Rather, we provide a brief introduction to the application terminology that you will encounter and to the features that we consider indispensable to portfolio development.

PowerPoint is primarily intended for use in developing presentations that will be projected onto a large screen for viewing by a group. Portfolio development is an adapted use. Portfolio viewing is usually done up close on a personal computer screen by a single individual or small group. This difference has implications for how slides are designed, for the amount of content that is presented on a slide, and for font size (see the discussion on design tips above).

If you are new to PowerPoint, some of its terminology may be unfamiliar to you. An example of this is the term *slide*. PowerPoint uses *slide* instead of *page* to indicate where, and on what, the document content is depicted. We use the term *slide* when referring to pages in an e-portfolio.

Layout is another term with which you need to be familiar. A slide layout includes boxes for text and boxes for objects, such as clip art, photographs, and charts. The slide layout controls placement of your content. PowerPoint provides a number of preprogrammed layouts from which to choose. These layouts can be changed and rearranged to suit your design purpose. Power-Point also gives you the flexibility to construct your own layouts using blank slides. Figure 7-13 is an example of a layout. It includes a box for the heading, a box for text, and a box for an object, in this case, clipart.

COMPETENCY 3 – PART II
HOW ARTIFACT DEMONSTRATES COMPETENCY
CFS 114: Child Crisis and Community Resources

- The completed research project focused on a case study of a specific crisis.

- Documented intervention.

- Discussed effectiveness of intervention.

- Identified community resources.

- The research allowed me to question the definition to the specific crisis.

- And sparked a desire to research further Dr. B. D. Perry's work on "The Vortex of Vi l   " (1996)

Figure 7-13. Layout and Background, Example 1.

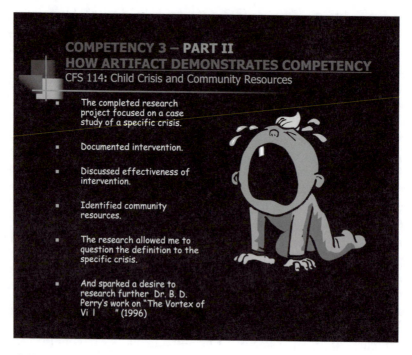

Figure 7-14.   Layout and Background, Example 2.

Another PowerPoint term that will be useful is *design template.* Like slide layouts, design templates are preprogrammed configurations that incorporate backgrounds and color schemes that you can choose to apply to individual slides or whole documents. Backgrounds range from solid colors to those that appear textured. They can also include graphics, from simple borders to full-slide pictorial images. These features, when used judiciously, lend continuity and interest to a portfolio. Figure 7-14 is the same slide as above using a design template.

E-portfolios are developed on two levels. We call the first level the *main-line.* Mainline slides (Figure 7-15) are those that are visually present in the main body of the portfolio. Either through auto-play or by manually scrolling through the portfolio, the reader can view each mainline slide. Many mainline slides may contain *hyperlinks.* Hyperlinks, also called links, connect the reader to slides anywhere within the mainline. Links that enable navigation within the mainline allow the reader to skip around the portfolio. The table of contents will contain links to each section of the portfolio.

The hyperlink feature also enables navigation between the mainline slides and support evidence stored in files outside of the PowerPoint structure. This use of hyperlinking allows the portfolio builder to create the equivalent of an appendix. We call this second level of the portfolio *linked documents.* This

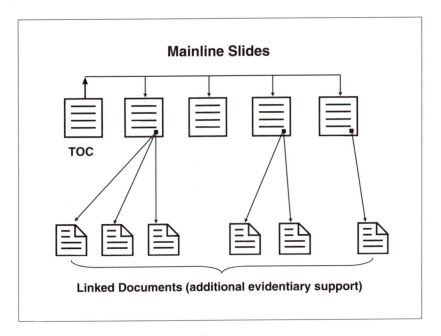

Figure 7-15.   Mainline Hyperlinked to Support Documents.

The hyperlink embedded in text looks like this: <u>Math Lesson.</u> It contains a word or phrase associated with the document.	The hyperlink in the form of an action button can be scaled to size. It looks like this: 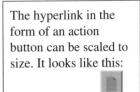

Figure 7-16.   Types of links: Underlined or Icon.

feature gives readers the option of going deeper into your work as their needs or interests dictate.

Hyperlinking is such an important feature in the development of e-portfolios that we have included instructions on how to do it. Links have two forms in PowerPoint. The first is a word or phrase inserted into the text where the hyperlink is needed. The second is an action button (Figure 7-16). It is important to note that action buttons are intended to be used in slide-show mode. They only work when the presentation is actually being shown, hence the word *action*. On a PowerPoint slide, the two forms look like those in the examples below.

Because portfolios are often burned (saved) to CDs or DVDs, we recommend the following steps as a matter of course when inserting hyperlinks (Figure 7-17).

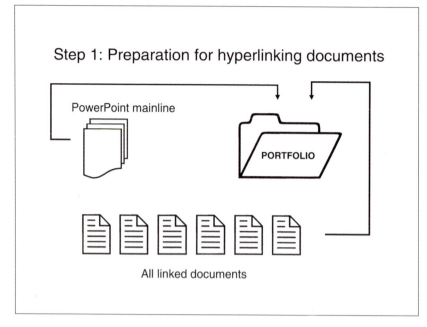

Figure 7-17.   Preparing for Hyperlinking Documents.

Step 1: Create a Master File

Create a file into which you save your PowerPoint mainline slides and all of the other files or documents to which you will create links. This step helps you avoid problems later when your link goes looking for files to open and cannot find them because they are scattered all over your hard drive.

After you have completed Step 1, you can begin inserting hyperlinks (Step 2a or 2b).

Step 2a: Create Hyperlinks in PowerPoint Slides

Open your PowerPoint mainline. Select the slide onto which the hyperlink will be placed. Place the cursor where you want the hyperlink on a particular slide. Type in the descriptor for the document to which you will link (e.g., Parent Handbook, Lesson Plan) and highlight it. Go to *Insert* on the toolbar, scroll down to *Hyperlink* and click. The descriptor you typed will appear in the *Text to Display* box. Use the *Browse* box to find your document, and double click on it. The descriptor you highlighted on your slide will become the link and will look like this <u>Parent Handbook</u>.

If you choose to insert action buttons instead of hyperlinks in text, as shown above, follow the steps in 2b.

Step 2b: Create hyperlinks using action buttons

Type a word or phrase onto your slide. Go to *Slide Show* on the toolbar, scroll to *Action Buttons* and select the button of choice. Place the crosshairs next to your word or phrase, hold down the left click side of the mouse, drag the cursor to size the button, and release.

In the *Action Settings* box, select *Hyperlink To* and scroll down to the appropriate choice. If you are linking to another slide within your mainline, select from choices such as *first slide, slide . . .,* or *next slide.* If you are linking to a document outside of the PowerPoint presentation, select *Other File.* Locate the file you want using the *Hyperlink to Other File* box. Select the file. The link is complete. It will look like this: ▣ Click here for Lesson Plan. Complete the linking process between all desired mainline slides and support documents in your portfolio.

Step 3: Create a Copy of Your Portfolio for Distribution

The moral of the story here is that, if you have taken care to create the master file as directed above, you can then burn the entire master file (PowerPoint mainline slides and all linked documents) to a CD or DVD *and keep your links intact!*

SCANNING DOCUMENTS FOR INCLUSION IN THE PORTFOLIO

Scanning is one of the ways that print documents and graphic images are converted to digital form. Scanning allows you to capture and save these items as digital files that can then be imported to the portfolio. It is the equivalent of photocopying for print portfolios. Hard copies of original documents, such as transcripts, letters of recommendation, photographs, and permits, will have to be scanned and saved in order for you to include them in your e-portfolio. Word-processed documents that are free of graphics can be saved as Word documents, and can be imported to PowerPoint as such. Documents bearing graphic images, such as photographs and permits, will need to be saved as JPEG files, since this is the format most readily recognized by PowerPoint. If you do not have access to a scanner, scanning services are available at many commercial outlets that provide business services. Photographs taken with digital cameras are automatically saved as digital files to the camera's storage media (e.g., memory card, memory stick). Once they are transferred from the storage device to a CD or to your computer's hard drive, they can be imported directly into PowerPoint as JPEG files. When scanning documents, it is frequently necessary to crop or otherwise enhance them in order to achieve a professional-looking result. If you are not familiar with scanning, you may need to seek technical assistance.

GENTLE REMINDERS

In this section, we present some suggestions related to writing conventions, organization, and tone that will enhance your portfolio's readability and appeal. While many of them may seem obvious, we have found that even the best writers benefit from an occasional reminder.

Writing Conventions

The portfolio represents you. As such, it is a tool that you can use to portray yourself as a competent communicator. All narrative statements, for example, the philosophy statement, explanations of artifacts, and reflections, should be well constructed, using standard English. You should write narratives in complete sentences with no errors in spelling, punctuation, grammar, or syntax. The exception to this is captions, which can be incomplete sentences but must be clear and descriptive. It is always a good idea to have someone proofread your documents. A fresh pair of eyes can pick up mistakes that you may have overlooked.

Organization

Make sure everything in the portfolio hangs together. Each entry's purpose and focus should be obvious. The reader should be able to follow your logic without difficulty and without asking questions such as, "Where did *that* come from?" or "What is this *connected* to?" A table of contents is a useful and necessary navigation tool and should be included regardless of portfolio type or format.

Tone

The tone you set in your portfolio will make an impression on the reader. Project a positive image. Look closely not only at what you say, but also how you say it. For instance, you might say, "I believe all children are capable of learning. A teacher's role is to individualize instruction so that every child works at his appropriate level." By contrast, a less positive way of saying this is, "I believe all children are capable of learning, but some will not be able to work at grade level because of their problems."

Tone also includes the use of person. Person reflects the degree of formality or familiarity used in your narrative. For example, when writing in the first person, the writer uses "I," as in "I believe . . ." It is appropriate in a portfolio to use the first person. After all, the portfolio is about you and what you can do.

Jargon is also an aspect of tone. Even though fellow educators are likely to be the readers of your portfolio, a good rule of thumb is to write as though the reader is unfamiliar with field-specific language, such as "zone of proximal development." Field-specific language includes acronyms. Even if you are sure the audience is familiar with the acronyms you use, always spell them out the first time they appear in your document. An example of an acronym often used in early care and education is DAP (developmentally appropriate practice).

A FINAL NOTE

As you have compared print and e-portfolios, you have noticed how similar they are in content and design and yet how they are constructed by very different methods. Whether you choose the print or electronic format, your goal should be to display high-quality content in a medium that communicates it effectively. Keep this mantra in mind: Quality content and communication! Show your stuff.

References

Arnett, J. J. (2004). *Adolescence and emerging adulthood* (3rd ed.). Upper Saddle River, NJ: Prentice Hall.

Badrova, E., & Leong, D. J. (1996). *Tools of the mind: The Vygotskian approach to early childhood education*. Columbus, OH: Prentice Hall.

Bartell, C., Kaye, C., & Morin, J. (1998, Winter). Portfolio conversation: A mentored journey. *Teacher Education Quarterly, 132.*

Brookfield, S. D. (1987). *Developing critical thinkers: Challenging adults to explore alternative ways of thinking and acting*. San Francisco: Jossey-Bass.

Brookfield, S. D. (1995). *Becoming a critically reflective teacher*. San Francisco: Jossey-Bass.

Brookfield, S. D. (1986). Teacher roles and teaching styles. In A. C. Tuijnman (Ed.), *International Encyclopedia of Adult Education and Training* (2nd ed.), Oxford: Elsevier Science, 529–534.

Brown, J. D., & Wolfe-Qunitero, K. (1997). Teacher portfolios for evaluation: A great idea or a waste of time? Retrieved from http://www.jaltpublications.org/tlt/files/97/jan/portfolios.html, accessed 9/24/01.

Bullard, J. (2003). Constructivism: Does your practice match your conceptual framework? *Journal of Early Childhood Teacher Education, 24*(3), 157–162.

Burk, D. I., & Dunn, M. (1996). Learning about learning: An interactive model. *Action in Teacher Education*, Summer, *18*(2), 11–18.

Campbell, D. M., Cignetti, P. B., Melenyzer, B. J., Nettles, D. H., & Wyman, Jr., R. M. (2004). *How to develop a professional portfolio: A manual for teachers* (3rd ed.). Boston: Pearson.

Candy, P. C. (1991). *Self-direction for lifelong learning*. San Francisco: Jossey-Bass.

Cerbin, W. (1994). The course portfolio as a tool for continuous improvement of teaching and learning. *Journal on Excellence in College Teaching, 5*(1), 95–105.

Curtis, D., & Carter, M. (2000). *The art of awareness: How observation can transform your teaching*. St. Paul, MN: Redleaf Press.

Daloz, L. A. (1999). *Mentor: Guiding the journey of adult learners*. San Francisco: Jossey-Bass.

DeVries, R., & Kohlberg, L. (1990). *Constructivist early education: Overview and comparison with other programs*. Washington, D.C.: National Association for the Education of Young Children.

Dewey, J. (1933). *How we think*. Boston: DC Heath and Company.

Dietz, M. E. (1995, Spring). Using portfolios as a framework for professional development. *Journal of Staff Development, 16*, 2, 40–43.

Erikson, E. (1963). *Childhood and society* (2nd ed.). New York: Norton.

Fink, L. D. (2003). *Creating significant learning experiences: An integrated approach to designing college courses*. San Francisco: Jossey-Bass.

Fosnot, C. (1996). Constructivism: A psychological theory of learning. In C. T. Fosnot (Ed.), *Constructivism: Theory, perspectives, and practice* New York: Teachers College Press, 8–33.

Froebel, F. (1826). *The education of man*. (W. N. Hailmann, Trans.). London: Appleton.

Frost, J. L., Wortham, S. C., & Reifel, S. (2005). *Play and child development*. New Jersey: Pearson.

Gardner, H. (1983). *Frames of mind: The theory of multiple intelligences*. New York: BasicBooks.

Goleman, D. (1994). *Emotional intelligence: Why it can matter more than IQ*. New York: Bantam Books.

Grant, G., & Huebner, T. (1998, Winter). The portfolio question: A powerful synthesis of the personal and professional. *Teacher Education Quarterly, 33.*

Harriman, P. L. (1941). Mental growth in children. In C. E. Skinner & P. L. Harriman, (Eds.), *Child psychology*. New York: The Macmillan Company.

Hillocks, George, Jr. (1999). *Way of thinking, ways of knowing*. New York: Teachers College Press.

Hutchings, P., & Wutzdorff, A. (Eds.). (1988, Fall). Knowing and doing: Learning through experience. *New Directions for Teaching and Learning, 35.* San Francisco: Jossey-Bass.

Hyson, M. (Ed.). (2003). *Preparing early childhood professionals: NAEYC's standards for programs.* Washington, DC: National Association for the Education of Young Children.

Katz, L. (1995). *Talks with teachers of young children: A collection.* Norwood, NJ: Ablex Publishing Corporation.

Kilbane, C. R., & Milman, N. B. (2003). *The digital teaching portfolio handbook: A how-to guide for educators.* Boston: Allyn and Bacon.

Langer, E. J. (1997). *The power of mindful learning.* Cambridge: Perseus Publishing.

Lyons, N. (Ed.). (1998). *With portfolio in hand: Validating the new teacher professionalism.* New York: . Teachers College Press.

McMillan, J. H. (2004). *Classroom assessment: Principles and practice for effective instruction* (3rd ed.). Boston: Pearson.

Mezirow, J. (1991). *Transformative dimensions of adult learning.* San Francisco: Jossey-Bass.

Mezirow, J., & Associates. (1990). *Fostering critical reflection in adulthood.* Oxford: Jossey-Bass.

Mezirow, J., & Associates. (2000). *Learning as transformation: Critical perspectives on a theory in progress.* San Francisco: Jossey-Bass.

Montgomery, K., & Wiley, D. (2004). *Creating e-portfolios using PowerPoint.* Thousand Oaks, CA: Sage Publications.

Paulson, F. L., Paulson, P. R., & Meyer, C. A. (1991). What makes a portfolio a portfolio? *Educational Leadership, 48* (5), 60–63.

Piaget, J., & Inhelder, B. (1969). *The psychology of the child.* New York: Basic Books.

Posner, G. (2005). *Field experience: A guide to reflective teaching.* Boston: Pearson.

Schon, D. A. (1983). *The reflective practitioner.* New York: Basic Books, Inc.

Strachey, J. (Ed. & Trans.). (1969). *An outline of psychoanalysis.* New York: W. W. Norton & Company, Inc.

Webb, L. D., Metha, A., & Jordan, K. F. (1992). *Foundations of American education.* New York: Macmillan Publishing Company.

Wilcox, B. (1996, November). Smart portfolios for teachers in training. *Journal of Adolescent & Adult Literacy, 40* (3), 172.

Wolf, K., & Dietz, M. (1998, Winter). Teaching Portfolios: Purposes and Possibilities. *Teacher Education Quarterly,* 9–22.

Wolf, K., Lichtenstein, G., & Stevenson, C. (1997, March). *Portfolios in teacher evaluation.* Paper presented at the Annual Meeting of the American Educational Research Association, Chicago, IL (ED 409 378).

Index